E

THE AENEID
BY
VIRGIL

Intelligent Education

INFLUENCE
PUBLISHERS

Nashville, Tennessee

BRIGHT NOTES: The Aeneid

www.BrightNotes.com

No part of this publication may be used or reproduced in any manner whatsoever without written permission, except in the case of brief quotations in critical articles and reviews. For permissions, contact Influence Publishers http://www.influencepublishers.com.

ISBN: 978-1-645425-24-3 (Paperback)

ISBN: 978-1-645425-25-0 (eBook)

Published in accordance with the U.S. Copyright Office Orphan Works and Mass Digitization report of the register of copyrights, June 2015.

Originally published by Monarch Press.

Julia Wolfe Loomis, 1964

2020 Edition published by Influence Publishers.

Interior design by Lapiz Digital Services. Cover Design by Thinkpen Designs.

Printed in the United States of America.

Library of Congress Cataloging-in-Publication Data forthcoming.

Names: Intelligent Education

Title: BRIGHT NOTES: The Aeneid

Subject: STU004000 STUDY AIDS / Book Notes

CONTENTS

INTRODUCTION TO VIRGIL

....

Publius Vergilius Maro was born in a small country village, Andes, near Mantua on October 15, 70 B.C. Tradition says his mother's name was Magia Polla, The daughter of a certain man of property, Magius, for whom Virgil's father worked at one time. From careful study of his poems and from references in early biographers, we learn that he was the son of a middle class farmer, received some education at the nearby city of Cremona, and possibly further education at Milan. He took his "graduate courses" in Rome and Naples, where the usual curriculum included rhetoric, philosophy, science and literature. He spent most of his adult life in Naples, but he incorporates into his poetry the most beautiful scenes from all the regions where he had lived. We have no definite knowledge of the events in his life until the year 42 B.C.

The battle of Philippi took place in October of that year between Julius Caesar's heirs, Antony and Octavius, and Brutus and Cassius (the old-guard faction, responsible for Caesar's assassination in 44 B.C.) To compensate the veterans of their victorious armies, Octavius and Antony confiscated land in the north of Italy. This was the very region where Virgil's father's farm was located. Through the influence of the governor of the territory, Asinius Pollio, Virgil was able to prevail upon Octavius to spare his father's farm. It is to this Pollio that he subsequently dedicated his first mature work, the *Bucolics*, or as they are more commonly called, the *Eclogues* (from the Greek word meaning "select poems"). These are short pieces about the joys and sorrows of idealized shepherds. There is evidence that Virgil lived both in Rome and in various country villas while he was composing the *Eclogues*. These were published around 37 B.C.

The next ten years of his life were occupied in writing his great work on farming, the *Georgics*. It is probable that they were first published about 30 B.C., and then revised in 26 B.C. (see introduction to *Georgics* for details). During much of this period the idea of writing a great **epic** was in the back of Virgil's mind. After the completion of the *Georgics*, he spent the rest of his life on the *Aeneid*. It was not yet ready for publication when in 19 B.C. he decided to take a trip to Greece and Asia Minor. He intended to devote three years there to the careful revision of the work. But while he was in Athens, he met Augustus who was returning to Rome to straighten affairs that had become out of hand during his four years absence from the capital. He persuaded Virgil to return with him. At Megara in Greece, Virgil caught a fever, and grew more and more ill during the voyage across the Adriatic Sea. He died on September 21, 19 B.C., shortly after his arrival in the port of Brundisium. He was not quite fifty-one years old.

Much has been written about Virgil's character and temperament. These works are opinions based on what each writer has felt most keenly through his own reading of the poems. The best way to understand Virgil is to read his works over and over again. He was a humble man who respected and admired the men in prominent positions who were his patrons: Pollio, Varus, Gallus, Maecenas, and finally the emperor Augustus himself. He had a burning sense of the importance of the mission of Rome. The beauty and history of his native land moved him deeply. Most important of all, he was filled with those yearnings which impel all great men: the desire for peace, the search after the nature of the divine and for inner contentment, and the longing to express one's beliefs in a form worthy of the greatest of his predecessors.

Table Of Gods And Goddesses: Greek and Roman Names

Greek Name	Roman Name	Function
Zeus	Jupiter	King of the gods
Hera	Juno	Queen of the gods, goddess of marriage and childbirth
Pallas Athena	Minerva	Goddess of wisdom
Poseidon	Neptune	King of the sea, patron of horses
Aphrodite	Venus	Goddess of love
Eros	Cupid	Son of Venus, god of love
Ares	Mars	God of war
Artemis	Diana	Goddess of the moon, of the hunt, and of chastity
Phoebus Apollo	Apollo	Sun-God, god of healing, patron of the arts
Demeter	Ceres	Goddess of seed-time and Harvest
Persephone	Proserpina	Queen of the underworld, daughter of Ceres
Hades	Pluto	King of the underworld
Kronos	Saturn	Father of Jupiter, Pluto, Neptune, ruler of the old order of gods
Hermes	Mercury	Messenger of the gods
Dionysus	Bacchus	God of wine
Hephaestus	Vulcan	God of fire

Dates in Virgil's Life
==

B.C.			42	Battle of Philippi
70	Birth of Virgil and Gallus		37	Publication of Eclogues
65	Birth of Horace		31	Battle of Actium
63	Birth of Octavius		27	Octavius assumes title of Augustus
59	Consulship of Caesar		26	Death of Gallus
55	Traditional death of Lucretius		22	Death of Marcellus
48	Battle of Pharsalia		19	Death of Virgil
48-44	Caesar supreme		A.D.	
44	Caesar's assassination		14	Death of Augustus

4

INTRODUCTION TO THE AENEID

The *Aeneid* is an **epic**. Webster's dictionary defines epic as follows: "A long narrative poem about the deeds of a traditional or historical hero or heroes of high station, such as the *Iliad* or *Odyssey,* with a background of warfare and the supernatural, a dignified style, and certain formal characteristics of structure (beginning in the middle of the story, catalogue passages, invocation of the muse, etc)." It is important to keep these points in mind in reading the *Aeneid,* but if we expect an exciting fulfillment of the first part of the definition, we shall be disappointed. The actual plot of the poem is weak. In fact, if the gods and goddesses did not interfere all the time, there would barely be any plot at all. Aeneas, the son of the goddess of love, Venus, and a prince of Troy, Anchises, escapes from the sack of Troy with a loyal group of fugitives. Their destination is Italy. They have a few insignificant adventures, mostly in the form of warnings about what to avoid.

They almost reach Italy but the queen of the gods, Juno, intervenes. She is angry that they have made the trip so easily, and sends a storm which drives them to Africa and the city of Carthage. There the hero meets the queen, Dido, makes love to her, and leaves her, because the king of the gods, Jupiter, tells him he must. He has a destiny, to found Rome. Aeneas obeys and sails away. Dido leaps on her burning funeral pyre, and dies.

The hero, after a short stay in Sicily and a trip to the underworld, eventually arrives in Italy. There the natives are friendly until Juno stirs them up. The fortunes of the ensuing war ebb and flow, but finally Aeneas kills the enemy's champion. There the story ends. The tale of the deeds of Aeneas, however, is not the main reason for the poem. Virgil wrote the *Aeneid* because he was obsessed with the idea of Rome's mission to the world. He wanted to create a work of art to rival the *Iliad* and *Odyssey* of Homer. He was a complex poet, and took as a skeleton the myth of Aeneas (which had existed in various forms for centuries) to convey the thoughts burning within him.

It is impossible not to compare the *Aeneid* with Homer's two epics. In such a comparison, however, the *Aeneid* always seems to suffer. This is because so many people think that Virgil's poem tried to be a combination of Homer's two, and failed. The hero, Aeneas, doesn't seem to be made of flesh and blood, as are Achilles and Hector, the great warriors of the *Iliad.* When we read Homer, we are right there with the leaders of both sides, Greek and Trojan. There is tremendous excitement. In the *Odyssey,* we accompany the clever scoundrel, Odysseus, on his adventures which equal the thrill of the Arabian Nights. However insurmountable the obstacle, odysseus always manages to come out on top. Aeneas, on the other hand, has really very few true adventures. He sails, he lands somewhere, and talks to someone who warns him about what will happen next. Except for his affair with Dido and his trip to the underworld, his so-called adventures are quite uneventful.

In Homer, the characters are men; in Virgil they are symbols first, and men only second. This brings us to the important point. The two poets can be compared, as they have been for centuries, and always will be. But if we come to a conclusion which says that the *Iliad* is full of life and vigor, and the *Aeneid* is slow and dull, we have totally missed the difference in the aims of the two poets. Homer's main purpose is to tell a story. Virgil's purpose is to show symbolically how Rome achieved her greatness. Both portray human character, but Virgil starts from the symbol and molds his characters to fit the symbol. Aeneas is symbolic both of the progress of Rome in history, and of Augustus' rise to the position of leader of the civilized world. Homer's heroes are examples of certain types of human character, but he did not consciously intend to make them symbols. Aeneas always acts fully aware of time past and time future, but hardly at all concerned with the present. Achilles and Hector, although a sense of tragedy hangs over them, are basically creatures of the present. We could go on enumerating differences. The point is that because Virgil built his poem on a Greek model, using his own original conception of the symbolic aspects of human character and history, he was able to create a work which not only added hitherto unknown depths to the power of the Latin language, but which appeals to us now as it did to the men of the Renaissance, and will to future generations.

We cannot leave the discussion of Virgil's models without a brief mention of two of the earlier Latin poets who wrote epics. Both their works exist only in such small fragments that a thorough comparison is not possible. The elder of these, Naevius, fought in the first war with Carthage (the First Punic War, 264-241 B.C.). When it was over he lived at Rome and wrote the story of the war as an **epic** poem. Its title was the *Punic War*. In the introduction he discussed the mythical origins of Rome and Carthage, Aeneas' escape from Troy, the storm at sea, Jupiter's promise to Venus concerning Rome's future greatness, Aeneas' visit to Dido's city, and the settlement of the Trojans in Latium. All of these elements are found in Virgil's poem. The rest of Naevius' work, however, dealt with the historical events of the Punic War itself.

The other early Roman writer of **epic** who influenced Virgil was Ennius (236-169 B.C.). Born in a small town, he served in the army, and eventually moved to Rome where he wrote poetry and plays. His **epic** of eighteen books was, like that of Naevius, based on history. It was called the *Annals*. The first book covered the period from the death of the king of Troy, Priam, to the deification of the founder of Rome, Romulus. Virgil's twelve books cover only part of Ennius' first one. The rest of the *Annals* was what we would call a history book about Rome. It could hardly be called a unified poem. Unfortunately we possess too little of these poets' works to discuss with any degree of certainty their similarities to Virgil. The great difference between Virgil and his Latin predecessors was that he transcended history by writing of myth, and thus gave his poem a universal application. Greek or Roman, he challenges all his models in the *Aeneid.*

Virgil probably commenced work on the poem before he completed the *Georgics.* In the introduction to the third Georgic he says that he is going to write an **epic**. Indeed, it was the great goal of his life. Perhaps he had composed a rough draft as early as 30 B.C. We have no way of knowing. But the rest of his life was occupied with the *Aeneid.* In 19 B.C. it was almost finished except for a few half lines and some passages he had not gone over. That year he planned a trip to Greece and Asia Minor where he intended to spend at least three years going over the work. He went as far as Athens where the emperor was staying on the last leg of his journey back to Rome. He persuaded Virgil to return to Italy with him. Before leaving Greece, Virgil fell ill. He lived only long enough to reach the Italian port of Brundisium. His dying wish was to have the poem destroyed because of its poetic imperfections, and inconsistencies in the plot. But Augustus ordered it published after Virgil's two literary executors had gone over it.

The poem consists of twelve books, the longest of which is 952 lines, the shortest, 705. The subjects of the books are as follows:

I. The invocation to the muse, the causes of Juno's anger, the wreck of Aeneas' fleet, and the arrival in Carthage where Aeneas meets Dido.

II. Aeneas' tale of the fall of Troy and his escape.

III. The tale of the adventures of the exiles on their voyage from Troy to Italy.

IV. The tragic love of Dido for Aeneas, the Trojan's departure from Africa, and Dido's death.

V. Festival of sports held in Sicily in honor of Aeneas' dead father, Anchises.

VI. Aeneas' visit to the prophetic Sibyl and his journey to the underworld.

VII. Landing in Latium in Italy, and Juno's rousing the native prince, Turnus, to fight the Trojans.

VIII. Aeneas' expedition up the Tiber to find allies in the war, his learning early Italian myths, and the start of the fighting while he is absent.

IX. Expedition of two Trojans, Nisus and Euryalus, to break through the enemy's camp and inform Aeneas of Turnus' attack, the burning of the Trojan ships, and Turnus' magnificent fighting.

X. The unproductive council of the gods, the return of Aeneas, and his search for Turnus whom Juno spirits away from the field of battle.

XI. Truce for both sides to bury their dead, the breaking of the treaty, and the renewal of fighting where the Trojans drive the enemy back within its own city walls.

XII. Encounter of the two champions, Aeneas and Turnus, and Turnus' death.

Virgil manipulates these characters and events to portray symbolically the whole history of Rome. He sees this history as an incorporation of three separate concepts:

1. the presence of the divine in men because of their ability to think and create lawful society;

2. the idea of heroes with a destiny;

3. the world of historical people and events.

At times he treats these concepts individually; at times they are woven together. It is this unique three-way vision of the poet, this ability to see human character and history symbolically, that enables Virgil to be ranked among the greatest poets of the world.

THE AENEID

BOOK I

The opening eleven lines of the *Aeneid* are a brief introduction in the **epic** tradition of Homer. Virgil announces that his story will concern the deeds and sufferings of a man (Aeneas) who is driven from Troy by destiny and a sense of divine duty. Aeneas' task is to found the city of Rome, but he is being kept from fulfilling this duty by the anger of the queen of the gods, Juno, the wife of Jupiter. Virgil appeals to the goddess of inspiration, the muse of poetry, to tell him the reasons for Juno's anger and to aid him in his great task of writing the poem.

Comment

Aeneas was a fugitive from the Trojan War and a native of Troy, which was located in north-eastern Asia Minor. He is now sailing somewhere in the Mediterranean with twenty ships on his way to Italy. Virgil mentions Troy in the introduction not only to recall the ancient legend that Rome's ancestors came from Asia Minor, but also to indicate his relation as a Roman poet to the Greek Homer, whose great **epic**, the *Iliad,* tells of the adventures of the Greek warriors in their attempts to capture Troy. But Aeneas is more than a hero such as Odysseus (whose wanderings after the Trojan War are told in Homer's *Odyssey).* Aeneas has a divine mission, symbolic of Virgil's conception of the divine mission of Rome. Aeneas' task is to found a city which will eventually be called Rome. Rome's mission is to govern the world with order and justice. This symbolic relation of Aeneas and Rome must be kept in mind through the whole poem, for otherwise Aeneas may seem to be a rather insipid sort of person and not at all like a hero. The poet alludes to the three steps in the founding of Rome when he mentions Latium, where Aeneas built the first city, Lavinium; Alba Longa, which was founded by Aeneas' son, Ascanius; and thirdly Rome, built by Romulus, a distant descendant of Ascanius.

The next seventy lines or so discuss the reasons for Juno's anger and her plan to get rid of the Trojans by having their ships destroyed in a storm. Juno is the patron deity of Carthage, a city located on the coast of Africa. It was founded by settlers from two Phoenician cities in Syria, Tyre and Sidon. (Historically this event took place around 800 B.C.) Juno wants Carthage to rule the world (instead of Rome) and decides to try and keep the Trojans from reaching their destined shore, Italy. If Rome is never founded, Juno thinks, then Carthage will have no rival; she has heard that if the city of Rome is built, descendants from that city will one day destroy her beloved Carthage. This is the first reason for her anger at the Trojans.

The second reason for her ire is that she was not selected when the Trojan prince, Paris, made the famous judgment as to which goddess was the most beautiful. The other two goddesses were Venus, the goddess of beauty and love, and Minerva, the goddess of wisdom. Venus was chosen the beauty-queen because she bribed Paris with a gift of the fairest mortal in the world, Helen. This is called the "Judgment of Paris."

A third was that the Trojans were descended from Jupiter, who was her husband, and another woman, a mortal. The final reason for Juno's anger was that Ganymede, a member of the royal house of Troy, was selected as the cupbearer of the gods, replacing her daughter Hebe. After enumerating these reasons for Juno's wrath, Virgil gives the reader a glimpse of the Trojan fleet sailing just beyond Sicily. We then go back to Juno, who decides to call a halt to their happiness. She goes to the king of the winds, Aeolus, to ask him to let loose the storm winds which he keeps chained in a cave. Juno is brooding all the while that she, the wife of Jupiter, should be allowed to cause storms if Minerva (Pallas Athena in Greek), who was only one of Jupiter's daughters, could cause them. To persuade him, Juno offers Aeolus a beautiful nymph (Diaopea). Aeolus consents, and strikes the mountain cave. The winds come shrieking out.

Comment

This passage is important because in it the reader meets the gods for the first time. To the poet Virgil, the function of the gods has two aspects: practical and symbolic. The practical aspect is that they serve to keep the story going by participating in the events. The symbolic aspect is that they serve to point up the various sides of human nature. Juno represents much that is bad: passion, anger, lack of control. On the other hand, Aeolus and Jupiter (whom we shall meet in the next passage) represent the control of the mind that leads to order. Virgil, and the whole Roman world of his time, was preoccupied with the idea of law and order because of the terrible period of disorder through which he had just lived: Italy had been plunged in Civil War for some eighty years preceding Octavius; victory at Actium in 31 B.C. where he defeated Anthony and Cleopatra. The reader must keep in mind the contrast of emotion and reason, violence and order in the *Aeneid*.

NAMES AND PLACES

Tiber: the river in Italy on which Rome is situated.

Samos: a Greek island in the Aegean Sea where an ancient temple to Juno was located.

Libya: used to mean all of Africa under Carthaginian rule.

Fates: refers to the three goddesses who controlled the thread of human life: Clotho held the spindle, Lachesis drew the thread, Atropos cut it.

Argos: one of the most important cities in Greece to supply fighters to Troy in the Trojan War. It is emphasized here because Juno had a great temple there.

Teucer: the mythical founder of Troy. Teucrian race is another way of saying Trojan, but it also indicates the Roman's reverence for their ancestors.

Ajax Son Of Oileus: (not the famous Ajax, son of Telemon, who plays an important role in the *Iliad*). His fleet was destroyed by Pallas Athena when he was returning from Troy; he had violated the prophetess, Cassandra (Priam's daughter) before the altar of Athena.

Aeolia: a small island northeast of Sicily. Referring to this island Virgil subtly reminds the reader of Homer's *Odyssey.* Odysseus, in his wanderings after the Trojan War, visited Aeolia. The king of the island, Aeolus, (as Homer tells the story) gave Odysseus a bag with all the storm winds tied up to insure favorable weather. After leaving, his companions, thinking it contained treasure, untied the bag. The ensuing storm brought on all Odysseus' troubles.

Tyrrhenian Sea: lies southwest of Italy.

Ilium: another name for Troy.

Gods: refers here to the household gods of the Romans, the Lares Penates. The Lares were the spirits of the dead who protected the home where they had lived. The Penates protected the food and material prosperity of the family. Images of the Lares and Penates were placed near the hearth, and at each meal offerings were made to them.

(LINES 81-156.)

Aeolus now releases the shrieking winds from the cave, and the resulting storm causes the destruction of Aeneas' fleet. In the midst of the thunder, lightning, surging sea, and black sky, Aeneas cries out in despair, wishing that he had died with his friends before the walls of Troy and the eyes of his parents. That would have been a noble death compared to drowning. But the storm grows worse. The oars break, three ships run afoul on the rocks, one ship goes down before Aeneas' very eyes, and all of them seem to be foundering. At this point the sea god, Neptune, becomes aware of what is going on. He is angered at Aeolus for causing a storm without asking his permission. With the aid of two lesser sea divinities, Cymothoe the sea nymph, and Triton the trumpeter, Neptune proceeds to undo the harm caused by Aeolus and his winds. The roaring ocean subsides and the remains of Aeneas' fleet make for the nearest shore (Africa). Virgil likens Neptune's calming of the storm to an orator who is able to sway and command huge crowds.

Comment

The preceding passage is important because here Aeneas enters the story. From his words in the depths of the storm we learn something of his character. First we learn that Aeneas is burdened by a sorrowful and loving memory of Troy. Yet he derives a strength from this memory which eventually enables him to found a new city. The speech, in a sense, for-shadows the development of Aeneas' character. Here Aeneas is only looking back to his past, but as the story unfolds we find Aeneas both looking back and looking to the future, and to the founding of Rome. The last step in his development occurs when he no longer looks back to Troy at all but is filled only with thoughts of Rome. The second thing we learn about Aeneas' character is his sense of filial devotion. This duty to and love of parents was a very important aspect of Roman life.

NAMES AND PLACES

Sarpedon: a son of Jupiter and a Trojan ally.

Simois: a small river near Troy.

Trident: a three-pronged spear, symbol of Neptune's power. Neptune was also the patron of horses and horseracing.

Simile: This word does not appear in the story but the comparison of Neptune with the orator is a **simile**. It is very important in the understanding of Virgil's art to notice how he uses these. Usually his **similes** are drawn from the natural or spiritual worlds. That is why this one is particularly interesting, for it seems to come from the Rome of Virgil's youth: in those strife-torn days when he was a boy, there were many orators who could sway the masses, such as the famous Cicero.

(LINES 157-222.)

At long last Aeneas and his friends reach land, though they do not know that the harbor they have come to is in Africa quite close to Carthage. Their first concern is to get themselves dried out and to find something to eat. Aeneas' closest friend, Achates, lights a fire, and everyone clusters around trying to dry out the waterlogged grain and corn. Aeneas, however, is worried about the thirteen lost ships, for only seven managed to reach the shore with him. Leaving the others by the fire he climbs a bluff to see what he can see. There is no sign of a ship anywhere, but a herd of deer feeding on the shore catches his eye. He proceeds to shoot seven of them, one for each ship. While they all eat their first decent meal in days Aeneas attempts to fill them with hope and renewed courage by making a brief speech, although he does not quite possess this hope and courage himself. He is terribly worried, not knowing where they are, or what has happened to all the others.

Comment

This passage reveals another important aspect of Aeneas' character, his greatness of soul. His comrades only vaguely understand his mission, so that he must comfort them and urge them on toward the great goal even though he is utterly miserable himself. Perhaps this points up the greatest contrast between the Homeric heroes and those of Virgil. Homer's heroes do what their human nature compels them to do, but Virgil's act to fulfill their sense of duty. Thus this speech, taken with his cry in the storm, shows the basic forces of Aeneas' nature: 1) his respect for duty, 2) his firm resolution, and 3) his understanding of the sufferings of others.

NAMES AND PLACES

Ceres: the goddess of harvest, crops, grain.

Phrygia: the ancient name for the country in Asia Minor where Troy was located. Here it is used instead of saying Troy.

Trinacrian Shore: Sicily; the name came from the fact that Sicily has three promontories and is triangular in shape.

Scylla: a six-headed monster who lived on the Italian side of the strait of Messina (the narrow bit of water that separates Italy from Sicily). She would snatch six men at a time off any ship that sailed near enough.

Cyclops: Polyphemus, a one-eyed giant who lived on the eastern side of Sicily.

(LINES 223-417.)

Meanwhile, back among the gods, it is Venus' turn to get upset. Aeneas is her son, and it seems to her that Jupiter has gone back

---

on his promise to help the Trojans. Tearfully she approaches the king of the gods and reminds him that the Trojans are his chosen people since they are to found Rome. Venus reproaches him with the fact that another Trojan, Antenor, found a refuge in the north of Italy. Why should not Aeneas, who is his own grandson? Jupiter, smiling at her concern, comforts her with a prophecy of Rome's future greatness, and sends the messenger of the gods, Mercury, (the son of Maia) to the Carthaginians. He persuades them to be hospitable to the Trojans.

The next morning Aeneas sets out to investigate his whereabouts and meets his mother (Venus) disguised as a huntress. He does not recognize her, though he is fairly sure she is not mortal, but he asks her where he is. Venus tells him that he has landed in Africa near Carthage and that the queen of the country is Dido. She then describes the whole story of Dido's flight from Tyre; how Dido's brother Pygmalion, murdered her husband, Sychaeus, so that Dido had to flee in secret. At the end of the story Venus asks Aeneas who he is (to keep up the deception), and when he mentions his lost ships she interrupts with the information that they are safe. Then she turns to go, and as a parting gesture, dissolves her disguise: the short huntress tunic falls down to her feet, perfume fills the air, and Aeneas recognizes his mother. He tries to keep her from going, but she vanishes after carefully veiling him and Achates in an invisible cloud. Concealed in this cloud, the two friends set out for Carthage.

Comment

The interview with Jupiter is an opportunity for Virgil to use one of his favorite poetic devices, contrast. Jupiter's unruffled calm is in sharp contrast to Venus' tears as well as a contrast to the tumult of the storm. The reader also becomes aware of the tremendous difference between the emotions of Jupiter and Juno. Jupiter is serene where Juno is passionate. But most important of all, the king of the gods is a symbol of what Rome, under Augustus, meant to Virgil. His powerful composure and kindly justice represent Rome's gift of law and order to the civilized world. Jupiter's speech gives Virgil his poetic opportunity to praise Rome and the great Augustus.

In addition to giving us a picture of Jupiter, this passage is important because in it occurs one of the most difficult words to put into English. That word is the adjective pius, rendered by many translators as good, and by a few as pious (its nearest English equivalent). Neither of these words is adequate because they make the reader think of Aeneas as a namby-pamby character. But to a Roman, the word pius was highest praise. It implied an eager willingness to fulfill one's duty to the gods, to parents, to the state, and to descendants. These duties were performed with a firmness of resolution which was noble and ungrudging. Thus the adjective pius and its corresponding noun, pietas, play a vital role in understanding the *Aeneid*.

NAMES AND PLACES

Illyria, Liburnia, the river Timavus: all located far up the Adriatic Sea. Antenor, escaping from Troy, sailed up the Adriatic and settled near Padua.

Caesar: here means Augustus. His whole name was Gaius Julius Caesar Octavius Augustus. Augustus, as Jupiter reveals toward the end of his speech, was made a god even before he died. In later times Roman emperors were usually not deified until after death.

Rutilians: the people living in Latium (in Italy) when Aeneas finally landed there. Aeneas had to defeat their King, Turnus, before he could settle.

Iulus: another name for Aeneas' son Ascanius. The play with the various forms of Iulus' name is to remind the reader of the Julian house and its ancestry. Thus Augustus, adopted by Julius Caesar, is related to Aeneas, the founder of the Roman race. (The Roman alphabet had no J, but I was used as both consonant and vowel. In Medieval times the consonantal I began to be written as a J.)

The Race of Hector: the Trojans, so named because Hector was their most famous hero.

Vesta: goddess of the sacred hearth fire which must always be kept burning. Her priestess, Rhea Silvia, was the mother (by the god Mars) of Romulus and Remus. (Her father was the king of Alba Longa, Numitor, descended from Ascanius.)

Phthia: the home of the great Greek hero, Achilles, in Thessaly.

Mycenae and Argos: the homes of Agamemnon, the leader of the Greek expedition to Troy, and Diomedes, both located in southern Greece. The whole region became a Roman province in 146 B.C.

Quirinus: another name for Romulus.

Gates of War: gates of the temple of Janus which were closed during times of peace, but open during war. Augustus closed them in 29 B.C. for the first time in nearly two hundred years. Janus was the early Italian god of entrances whose name is derived from the Latin word meaning door. He had two faces, one looking forward and the other back.

Harpalyce: a female warrior from Thrace.

Sist R of Phoebus Apollo: Diana, goddess of the moon. Her favorite sports were hunting and dancing.

Agenor: founder of Sidon, the sister city of Tyre.

Byrsa: the Greek word for bull's hide. Venus is describing the circumstances of the founding of Carthage. The colonists had been granted as much land as bull's hide could cover, so they cut the hide into thin strips and thus traced out a large piece of land.

Mt. Olympus: the home of the gods, located in Thessaly.

Ambrosia: usually the food of the gods, but here it is a perfume.

Paphos: a town on the west coast of Cyprus where a famous temple to Venus was located.

(LINES 418-755.)

Aeneas and his friend, Achates, still hidden in the cloud which Venus had thrown around them, make their way along a path till they finally reach Carthage. Here they admire the bustling energy of the workmen who are still engaged in building; they are compared in a great **simile** to bees around a hive. Arriving at Juno's magnificent temple, the two friends are filled with even greater admiration, as well as distress: for on the walls of the temple are huge murals depicting all the tragic events of the fall of Troy. Aeneas himself appears in one painting. While they are gazing, overcome with sorrowful memories, the queen of Carthage, Dido, comes to the temple. She is accompanied by a great throng of citizens and princes, and behind them are the rest of Aeneas' followers from the thirteen lost ships. As Venus had promised him, they are safe. But of course no one sees Aeneas and Achates enfolded in their cloud!

After Dido has taken her seat near the temple door, various citizens approach her and make requests. She dispenses justice with calm dignity. Then the leader of the group of men from the lost ships, Ilioneus, comes forward from his position. He complains of inhospitable treatment on the part of the Carthaginians, and says that he and his men are not looters or warriors. He begs permission to repair the battered ships so that they can be on their way. Dido apologizes, promising to help them, and even offers to let them stay in Carthage. At that moment, Aeneas, unable to stand it any longer, bursts out of his enveloping cloud and reveals himself. With a heart overflowing with gratitude, he begs the gods to reward Dido, the first person to show any pity and love for the Trojans. Dido responds graciously by inviting them all to a banquet at the palace. Immediately Aeneas sends Achates back to the ships to get everyone who was left behind, and especially to fetch his son, Ascanius.

But Venus, who has been keeping an eye on what has been going on and is still worried that Juno may try some new trick, decides that, for the Trojans to be really safe, Dido must fall in love with Aeneas. To accomplish this romance, she commands her son, Cupid, to assume the disguise of Ascanius (who is still a small boy). In the meantime she puts the real Ascanius to sleep. So Achates returns to the city, not with Ascanius, but with Cupid. The false Ascanius embraces his "father" and then climbs on Dido's lap. Poor Dido hasn't a chance! All during the banquet, and while the various Carthaginian princes are singing their ballads, she cannot take her eyes off Aeneas. Finally she persuades him to tell the story of his adventures during the seven years from the fall of Troy till he landed in Carthage. And with this forecast of the contents of Book II, the first book of the *Aeneid* comes to a close.

Comment

The closing portion of Book I contains two important poetic devices. The first of these, the **simile**, we have already met twice before. The third **simile** concerns one of Virgil's favorite subjects, bees. His great study of their habits occurs in the fourth book of the *Georgics*. The second device is the telling of the background of the story by means of pictures or reminiscence. Thus the past can be explained without breaking the thread of the present, while the reader gains a greater understanding of Aeneas' sorrows. Virgil in the murals is also recalling Homer, not only by referring to the chief characters of the *Iliad*, but also by echoing Homer's description of Achilles' shield with his own description of the murals. Virgil never ceases to be conscious of writing within the **epic** framework established by Homer.

NAMES AND PLACES

Sons Of Atreus: Agamemnon and Menelaus, the chiefs of the Greeks together with Achilles, in the Trojan war. But Achilles refused to fight at first because he was angry with Agamemnon for taking his captive princess from him.

Rhesus: a Thracian king who was supposed to help the Trojans. An oracle had prophesied that the Greeks could not take Troy if the horses of Rhesus were to eat the grass around Troy and drink from its chief stream, the Xanthus. Unfortunately, Rhesus was killed by the Greeks and his horses seized by Odysseus and Diomedes (the son of Tydeus).

Troilus: youngest son of Priam, king of Troy. He was killed by Achilles. The scene concerning Hector refers to Priam's ransoming Hector's body after Achilles had dragged it three times around the walls.

Memnon: led the Ethiopian allies of Troy.

Amazons: a warrior nation of women whose queen, Penthesilea, came to the aid of the Trojans. She too was slain by Achilles.

Eurotas: a river near Sparta in southern Greece.

Mt. Cynthus: located on the Greek island of Delos and one of Diana's favorite spots. From the name of the mountain comes the other most common name of Diana, Cynthia. Her followers were the mountain nymphs, the Oreads.

Hesperia: means Italy. The word is Greek for "Western Land."

Oenotria: another name for Italy, "Land of Vines."

Orion: the constellation which in the middle of summer rose near sunrise, and was thought to cause storms.

Acestes: king of Sicily. He was friendly to the Trojans because his mother came from Troy.

Tyrian Town: Carthage, since it was founded by settlers from Tyre.

Fields Of Saturn: a third name for Italy because Saturn was supposed to have ruled Italy in the Golden Age.

Eryx: another son of Venus. The country of Eryx means Sicily because Eryx, when king of Sicily built a temple to Venus on a mountain in the western part of the island.

Paros: a Greek island in the Aegean Sea which provided the most beautiful white marble in antiquity. The passage in which this word occurs is an echo of lines 156-162 from Book XXIII of the *Odyssey*. Virgil has Aeneas emerging from the cloud; Homer has Odysseus emerging from the bath when he has finally reached his home. Both are clad in dazzling beauty by a goddess. Virgil, of course, assumes that his readers know the works of Homer.

Teucer: not the founder of Troy here, but one of the sons of Telamon and a nephew of Priam. (His mother was Priam's sister, Hesione). When Teucer returned from Troy without his half-brother, Ajax, Telamon banished him to Cyprus. On the way he stopped off at Sidon to arrange terms with Belus (Dido's father) who was ruler of Cyprus.

Pelasgian: means Greek here, although the term actually refers to the race which inhabited Greece in pre-historic times before the Greeks arrived.

Helen: the famous wife of Menelaus, king of Sparta, who ran off with Paris, prince of Troy. Sparta was located in the Argive plain, as was Mycenae (ruled by Agamemnon).

Pergamum: the citadel, or inner stronghold, of Troy.

Typhoeus: a giant placed beneath a volcano by Jupiter's thunderbolts.

Cythera: an island off the southeastern part of Greece where a famous temple to Venus was located. Although some legends said she rose from the sea near Paphos, others said it was near Cythera.

Idalium: a town in Cyprus sacred to Venus.

Acidalian Mother: Venus; the name came from the fountain, Acidalius, in Boeotia (central Greece) sacred to Venus and her followers, the three Graces.

Bacchus: the well-known god of wine, whose favorite home was Thrace.

Bitias: a Carthaginian noble.

Topas: another noble who was supposed to have been taught by Atlas, the legendary first astronomer. The mountain in northwestern Africa was named after him. Iopas' **ballad** concerns the eclipses of the sun. The ancients referred to them as "the toils of the sun" because they thought the sun was enduring great struggles at such a time.

Arcturus, Hyades, Bears: three constellations. The Hyades were associated with rainy weather.

Aurora's Son: Memnon; Aurora, goddess of the Dawn, married Priam's brother, Tithonus.

SUMMARY

The first book of the *Aeneid* serves to introduce several of the most important characters in the poem and to reveal its basic themes.

1. We learn something of the personality of Aeneas. This personality is to grow and change with the development of the **epic**: his sorrowful memory of the events in Troy and his yearning for the past; his noble spirit looking forward to Rome, shown by his willingness to undergo all trials in order to fulfill the destiny set by the gods; and his human feeling for the sufferings of others.

2. We learn a little about Dido's generosity and her impulsive actions of the heart. The appearance of Cupid is a **foreshadowing** of the love story which is told in detail in the fourth book.

3. We are introduced to the various roles of the gods: a.) Jupiter, the unruffled dispenser of law and order; b.) Juno, the goddess with unruly emotions, jealousy, anger, passionate love for her chosen people, the Carthaginians; c.) Venus, the watchful mother and protectress of Aeneas; d.) Neptune, powerful like his brother Jupiter, but not quite as serene, also on the side of the Trojans.

4. Lastly, the poet reveals his themes.

   a. The greatness and mission of Rome, symbolized by Aeneas, and given special emphasis by the fact that Rome is the last word in the first five introductory lines to the poem.

b. The contrast of violence with order, emotion with self-control, seen in the personalities of the gods and mortals, and even in nature itself.

c. The continuous awareness of the greatness of Homer. achieves this awareness by subtle references to the *Iliad* or *Odyssey,* or by almost word for word translations. However, Virgil has a concept of the Homeric tradition which he develops with a more spiritual insight. For Homer's heroes are pretty much men of the moment who act as their natures make them, but Virgil' characters always carry with them a sense of past and future, and act from duty, the noblest of Roman virtues.

THE AENEID

BOOK II

. . . .

(LINES 1-249.)

The events of Books II and III are a flashback from Book I. In them Aeneas relates the tragedy of the fall of Troy (II) and the fortunes of the exiles on land and sea after they flee from Troy (III). At the end of the first book we left Aeneas when the banquet was over with an audience of Carthaginian nobles, waiting spellbound to hear his tale about the fall of Troy.

After ten years of fighting and getting nowhere, the Greeks, pretending to be discouraged, had withdrawn to the island of Tenedos, off the coast of Troy. They had left behind them, however, a huge wooden horse. When the Trojans, thinking the Greeks has sailed away, rushed out of the city with joy to see the abandoned camp they found the horse and were at a loss as to what to do. Some were for drowning it in the sea, others wanted to drag it into the city. The strongest voice against the horse was raised by the priest Laocoon. Ending his speech with the famous words "I fear the Greeks, even when they bring gifts," he hurled his spear at the horse's side. A great echo came forth, like a moan, but the rest of the Trojans were not convinced. And just at this point of indecision, some shepherds rushed forward with a young Greek prisoner.

Little did the Trojans suspect what trickery the Greeks could think up. For this man, Sinon, had let himself be captured so that he might persuade the Trojans to not fear the horse. Weaving a tall tale, Sinon told Priam (king of Troy) how it was that he came to be hated by Ulysses (Odysseus is his Greek name): Ulysses with his clever words had managed to persuade the sooth-sayer, Calchas, that Sinon was the cause of the Greeks' misfortunes in battle. When Calchas had appealed to the oracle of Apollo to ask what should be done, the answer came that just as the Greeks appeased the winds with the blood of a virgin (see under comment) in order to get to Troy, so another life must be sacrificed in order to leave. Obviously Sinon was the man. This was the reason for his running to the protection of Priam. The old king was completely taken in by the dreadful story, and begged Sinon to explain the existence of the horse. Swearing up and down that he hated the Greeks and would always hate them, Sinon said that the horse was an offering to Minerva (her Greek name is Athena). Minerva had been offended when Diomedes and Ulysses had touched her small wooden image (Palladium) with bloody hands and therefore caused the Greek fortunes to fall. To atone for this crime and to regain the goddess' favor, Calchas had told them to make a gigantic horse out of wood so big that the Trojans would not be able to get it inside their city wall. The poor Trojans believed every word.

To their horror, they then saw two huge serpents coming through the waves and heading straight for them as they were gathered around Laocoon, who was preparing to sacrifice a bull to Neptune. In a panic everybody fled, except Laocoon and his two sons. The serpents coiled around the two sons and choked them to death. Moments later Laocoon shared their fate, and their screams filled the air. To all the Trojans this seemed a sign that Minerva was angry with Laocoon for denouncing the horse, and so with much celebration and singing they dragged it into the city. Even then, there was one last chance to save themselves. Cassandra, Priam's daughter, rushed out to prophesy the dreadful things to come. But when Apollo had given her the ability to prophesy he cursed her at the same time because she had rejected him as a lover. The curse was that no Trojan would ever believe her. Little realizing the terrible events that would come with nightfall, the happy Trojans wreathed the temples of the gods throughout the city with garlands.

Comment

Book II commences at a swift pace which gathers momentum as the battle scenes are portrayed and follow one another in swift **imagery**. It is a book of scenes, but it is a book containing individual portraits as well. In this first passage we have no trouble in imagining to ourselves either the traitor Sinon, or the tortured Laocoon. (In fact the vivid account in Virgil of the death-agony of father and sons was the subject of one of the most famous sculptures of the second half of the first century by three Rhodian sculptors, Agesander, Athenodorus, and Polydorus).

NAMES AND PLACES

Myrmidons and Dolopians: soldiers of Achilles from Thessaly.

Ulysses: known in Homer as "wily Odysseus" or Odysseus of many schemes" went through many years of wandering around various parts of the Mediterranean after the Trojan war. Aeneas is therefore drawing a subtle comparison with his own adventures. Ulysses is also credited by legend with being the author of the plan for the wooden horse. His home was the island of Ithaca.

Danaans: another poetic name for the Greeks, coming from the name of one of the early kings of Argos, Danaus.

Achaeans: another tribe of Greeks, dominant in the southern part. The word is often used by Virgil to mean all the Greeks.

Dardanian: equals Trojan, from Dardanus, a mythical ancestor of the Trojans.

Palamedes: earned Ulysses' hatred by proving that Ulysses was not mad. Ulysses, not wishing to join the expedition for Troy had pretended insanity. As evidence, he yoked a horse and a bull together to plough the seashore. Then he sowed it with salt. Clever Palamedes placed Ulysses' son, Telemachus, in the furrow, and Ulysses, seeing him, turned aside. To get his revenge, Ulysses later forged a letter from Priam to Palamedes which arranged for the latter to betray the Greeks. As further proof Ulysses hid some gold in Palamedes tent. Palamedes was therefore found guilty and put to death.

Belus: son of Neptune, father of Aegyptus and Danaus, who, according to some traditions was king over Libya and Egypt.

The Virgin: Iphigenia, daughter of Agamemnon, was sacrificed to Diana at Aulis (on the strait of Euboea) in order that the Greeks might have fair winds to Troy.

Son of Tydeus: Diomedes.

Omens: Here Virgil is imposing the Roman custom of consulting the auspices on a Greek priest. It consisted of examining the entrails of animals or of observing the way chickens pecked at corn which was thrown to them. The Romans rarely did anything without consulting auspices or omens. A tremendous amount of ritual was involved, and one little wrong step meant that the whole thing had to be done again.

Tritonia: Minerva.

(LINES 250-558.)

Night descended and inside the city everyone slept, believing that the Greeks had truly departed. They could not have been more wrong. The Greek fleet sailed stealthily in the moonlight back from Tenedos, where it had been hiding, to the Trojan shore. When the commander's ship had given the signal light, Sinon, who had been watching from within the walls, opened up the wooden horse and they proceeded directly to kill the men on watch and throw wide the gates to the rest of the Greeks. Meanwhile (Aeneas now brings himself into the story) the dead Trojan hero, Hector, appeared to Aeneas in a dream and warned him to escape. He must not even think of trying to organize a defense, as Troy was in flames. His parting words were to take his household gods, the Lares and Penates, with him as symbols of Troy to the new city which he was to establish.

But while Aeneas dreamt, Troy burned, and rousing himself hastily from sleep (as the hero tells us), he rushed out on the roof. The description of the fire is the chance for Virgil's first **simile** in Book II: picture a beautiful cornfield in flames while the wind rages; or imagine a flooded river pouring destruction on fields and flocks while from a safer, higher spot, the shepherd looks on helpless. Aeneas too, was helpless. As he stood there, a friend, Panthus, came up with the news that the Greeks were masters of Troy. This information so inflamed Aeneas that he dashed out into the fighting on the city streets, gathering a small group of loyal hearts as he went. Virgil compares these last brave Trojans to a pack of wolves, wild with long hunger. Thus they fought their way to the center of the city. There they met a band of Greeks who mistook them at first for friends. Too late they realized the error. The Greek leader, Androgeos, jumped back as if he had suddenly stepped on a snake. Aeneas and his group slaughtered the Greek band and took their armor.

So the battle surged till they came to the thickest part of the fighting around Priam's palace. No matter how many Greeks were killed by the missiles falling and being thrown, they still kept coming. Finally a Greek leader, Pyrrhus whom Virgil compares to a viper fed on poisonous herbs, sleek and slippery, forced the inner door and the horde swarmed into Priam's palace. Here Virgil again uses the comparison of a river swollen into a flood and overwhelming its banks to give vividness to the picture of the rush of the Greeks. Priam's wife Hecuba, together with her daughters, was slain beside the household altar. As the aged king himself was struggling to reach her and the sanctuary of the altar, one of his sons, Polites, fled by, trying to escape the word of Pyrrhus. Right in front of Priam, Pyrrhus caught up with his victim and stabbed him to death. Filled with anger and despair the weak king in vain hurled his spear, which of course bounced harmlessly off Pyrrhus' shield. Then slipping and sliding in the son's gore, Pyrrhus grabbed the old father by the hair of his head, and buried his sword up to the hilt in the king's body. Then he struck off the head and left the body there, a "corpse without a name."

Comment

This passage presents powerfully striking images and a sense of immediacy to the reader. In achieving this result, the **similes** play a very important role. There are six **similes** in little more than two hundred and fifty lines. Another way Virgil creates immediacy is by making his individual descriptions brief and by jumping quickly to the next. It is an effect similar to that of the modern movie camera in "swish-pan" shooting where the camera focuses on one spot and then swishes along the horizon line to the next, leaving the intervening objects in a rushed blur to show that the two focused scenes are connected. This passage is also important in giving us the only picture of Aeneas before the awesome burden of his destiny fills his life. Here he is like one of Homer's heroes, eager for battle in spite of impossible odds.

NAMES AND PLACES

The Spoils of Achilles: Hector killed Patroclus who was wearing Achille's armor. The armor of a dead man belonged to his slayer.

Penates: Aeneas took with him his own household gods, but these represented those of Troy. Hector also entrusted him with an image of Vesta, the goddess of the never-dying hearth fire.

Deiphobus: the third of Priam's sons (Hector and Paris were the oldest). He married Helen after Paris was slain in battle, and therefore his house was the first to burn.

Pergamum: the inner stronghold of Troy.

Orcus: the god of Death and also the Underworld, sometimes referred to as Pluto.

Andromache: wife of Hector. Their first-born son was named Astyanax, which in Greek means "lord of the city." One of the most touching scenes to modern readers in the *Iliad* is the description of Hector's farewell to his wife and son at the gates of the city. (Book VI, 370 ff.)

Pyrrhus: his other name is Neoptolemus. He was the son of Achilles, sent for after his father was killed by Paris, with Apollo's help.

Scyros: an island in the Aegean which was the kingdom of Pyrrhus' grandfather, Lycomedes.

(LINES 558-804.)

It was the horrible sight of Priam's death which brought Aeneas up short. He had been filled only with the rage to kill and to get even. But the violent death of the beloved king brought the image of Aeneas' own aged father to his mind. For the first time, also, he thought of his wife, Creusa, and their son Iulus. Looking around, he found himself deserted, and then suddenly spied the cause of all the trouble, Helen, daughter of Tyndareus. In terror of the Trojan's anger, she was hiding behind the altar. With a frenzied mind, Aeneas started for her, with intent to kill. But his ever watchful mother, Venus, appeared in a vision, radiantly beautiful, and prevented him with words about his father and his family. She told him that it was the ill-favor of the gods, not Helen or even Paris who had caused the destruction of Troy. The very gods themselves were taking sides with the Greeks: Neptune, Juno, Minerva, Jupiter. Aeneas looked around. The fall of Troy was like (and here follows one of Virgil's most famous similes) a huge tree on the top of the mountain which woodsmen have hacked away at for hours which finally crashes down with its roots all torn up.

BRIGHT NOTES STUDY GUIDE

But amid all the flames and fighting, Aeneas, under divine protection, made his way safely back to his own home. At first his father refused to be rescued, claiming that he was too old and had lived long enough. The whole house burst into tears trying to persuade him, but to no avail. Finally Aeneas started to rush off into the fighting again, and Creusa, holding up the small son in her arms, begged him at least to let them die with him. But as she spoke a miraculous omen occurred. A tiny flame appeared over Iulus' head and set his hair on fire. But the holy flames did not hurt him, although the anxious mother put them out as quickly as she could. To the old father, Anchises, however, it was a sign. He resisted the entreaties of his son no longer. Two other omens followed: a thunderbolt and a shooting star. Without wasting any more time, Aeneas took his father on his shoulders and his son by the hand, while Creusa followed behind. Their destination was a small hill outside the city where an ancient temple of Ceres stood. To prevent Aeneas' pollution of the sacred household images (since he had just come from battle) Anchises was to carry them. But the story was not to have such a happy ending. For Aeneas, hearing the sound of pursuing Greeks close at hand, took a few back alleys and shortcuts, and arrived at Ceres' temple; only Creusa was not with them.

Leaving his father and son there, Aeneas, totally distraught, retraced his steps back to the burning city, calling loudly for Creusa. There was no answer. Suddenly, Creusa's ghost appeared and told him it was not the will of the gods that she should go with him. He would find a royal wife in Hesperia (Italy) and a fortunate turn of events; even a kingdom. Her last words were to take care of their child. Aeneas tried to put his arms around her but she vanished, and there was nothing else for him to do but to go back to his father and son and the other Trojans who had gathered with them. Thus Aeneas shouldered his burden of leadership, and the exiles departed.

Comment

In this passage we see one of Virgil's most important poetic affects, the swift change of mood. Up to the death of Priam we have been conscious only of the glory of war. Even the burning city is something splendid. But after the brutal slaying of the king of Troy, we become conscious only of the horror of war. It is this sense of horror that forces Aeneas to surrender himself to his destiny, which was first foretold him by Hector in the dream and later repeated by the ghost of Creusa. Aeneas has thus changed from a Homeric hero living almost entirely in the present, to a Virgilian hero constantly aware of both past and future.

NAMES AND PLACES

Tyndareus: husband of Leda but not actually Helen's father. Leda was her mother, Jupiter her father.

Furies: the avenging deities of crimes toward parents, murder, and the like. They were said to take away all peace of mind and to lead their victims to wretched misfortune. (The Greek word for them is Erinyes).

Neptune: not only the sea god, but the builder of Troy for Laomedon. Now he is going to help destroy his creation.

Scaean Gate: the most important gate into Troy.

Phoenix: Achilles' aged tutor.

Lydian Tiber: Tradition holds that the area around the Tiber and just north of it, where the Etruscans lived, was colonized by the Lydians from Asia Minor.

Mother Of The Gods: Cybele, the Great Mother goddess of Asia Minor. She is also known as Rhea.

SUMMARY

Book II has two important functions. 1.) In it Virgil reveals his ability to create scenes that are immediately visible to the imagination of the reader. We are consistently aware of the turmoil of battle and the determination of the warriors. 2.) The second function of the book is to make the reader realize what a horrible memory it is that Aeneas has to carry with him on his long journey to found a new city. The fierce heat of the flames, the screams, the lost wife, the king slaughtered in the still warm blood of his son, all these were ever present in Aeneas' mind. No wonder the process of forgetting took so long. The ability to lay these aside, and the courage and dedication to go on to build a city with a mighty future, make Aeneas a great hero.

THE AENEID

BOOK III

. . . .

(LINES 1-293.)

Book III continues the flashback begun in Book II. Aeneas is still relating the story of what happened after the collapse of Troy. By early summer Aeneas and the few men who had managed to escape the burning city had constructed a fleet. In ancient times no one ever sailed directly across an open body of water if it were possible to sail close to the coast. So the first place they landed at was Thrace, which has long been friendly to Troy. There Aeneas founded a city Aeneadae. But as he was about to sacrifice to Venus and was starting to pull up some saplings of myrtle to garland the altar, blood seemed to drip from the bark. Then came a moan and a voice asking why was he disturbing the grave of Polydorus, who had been sent by his father Priam to the king of Thrace. When Agamemnon conquered and the power of Troy was no longer great, the Thracian king had slain him. Because of such a dreadful omen, it was quite obvious to Aeneas that they could not stay where they were any longer.

After performing new funeral rites to quiet the unhappy ghost, the Trojan exiles took to their ships again.

The next shore they reached was the island of Delos, birthplace of Apollo and Diana. There the king, Anius, welcomed them and Aeneas sought the advice of Apollo's oracle. As was usual, the oracle's answer was not very clear: he was to seek out the land from which their race had originally sprung. Anchises assumed that this meant Crete because there was a Mt. Ida on Crete as well as near Troy. Legend also said that Teucer, the founder of the Trojan race, came from Crete to Troy. Joyfully the Trojans left Delos and with a following breeze they soon sighted the coast of Crete.

A second time they set to work to build a city. This time they named it Pergamum after the inner citadel of Troy. But misfortune was not far off. A dreadful disease attacked both men and crops, accompanied by scorching drought. Anchises advised them to return to Delos and obtain another oracle. But one night in a dream the sacred household gods which Aeneas had brought from Troy appeared to him and told him that the promised land was Hesperia, otherwise known as Italy. It filled the qualifications of being the land from which the founder of the Trojan race came because Iasius, who was born in Italy, had married one of Teucer's daughters. When Aeneas revealed this dream to his father, Anchises recalled that Cassandra had prophesied that Italy was their goal. But of course, due to Apollo's curse, no one had ever believed her.

Again they set sail and after a storm which lasted three days and nights they sight land: the two islands of the Strophades in the Ionian Sea, west of Greece. Bad luck was to be followed by worse, for these islands were inhabited by winged creatures with women's faces, known as Harpies. Whatever they touched became unclean. Thus when Aeneas and his followers killed some of the goats and cattle they found feeding on the grass (they probably had little if anything to eat during the three day storm and were ravenous) the Harpies swooped down and contaminated everything, including the sacrifice on the altar. Hastily Aeneas told everyone to try and fight the winged things off. The hideous creatures flew away, but their leader, Celaeno, paused on a high cliff to curse them. She cried that they would reach Italy, but that they would not build the walls of their city till hunger forced them to devour the very tables on which they ate. Everyone wanted to leave such a horrible place as quickly as possible, so they hastily got underway.

After sailing up the western coast of Greece past the island home of Ulysses, Ithaca, they made a brief stop at Actium. There they held a festival of games and wrestling, and then pushed on further north till they came to Chaonia, where they found friends.

Comment

In this passage the reader cannot help but have a slight feeling of unreality about the serious nature of Aeneas' adventures. Perhaps this is because Virgil, in trying to follow Homeric footsteps, did not really believe these adventures would increase the greatness of his hero. Whatever the reason, the events somehow lack the vividness of the scenes in Book II.

NAMES AND PLACES

Lycurgus: persecuted Bacchus and his kingdom therefore became sterile; its fertility returned after his exposure on a mountain.

Dione: daughter of Earth and Sky, loved by Jupiter, and thus mother of Venus.

Nymphs: the Hamadryades, or nymphs of the groves who lived in trees. They symbolized the spirit of the tree for they were born with it, and died when it died. As lesser goddesses, Aeneas first worships them, and then Gradivus (Mars) the more important divinity of Thrace. (Getic means Thracian, since the Getae were one of the Thracian tribes.)

Nereids: There were fifty of them, nymphs of the Mediterranean, daughters of Doris and Nereus.

Gyaros And Myconos: two islands in the group known as the Cyclades. Legend runs that Apollo was supposed to have moored Delos, because it was so tiny to the two larger islands of Gyaros and Myconos.

Phoebus: another name for Apollo.

Thymbra: a place near Troy where Apollo had a famous temple.

Rhoetean: here means Trojan after the name of a small promontory north of Troy called Rhoeteum.

Cybele: a mountain, sacred to the goddess of the same name, located in Phrygia.

Corybantes: followers of Cybele who performed her rites with clashing cymbals and wild dancing. Lions were harnessed to her chariot.

Gnossos: (Knossos in Greek spelling) the most important city in Crete.

Zephyrus: the west wind.

Idomeneus: Cretan leader who took part in the Trojan war. On his way home a storm came up and he foolishly vowed to Neptune the first living creature that he should meet if he arrived safely. Naturally the first thing he met was his son. Obediently he sacrificed him, but a plague followed. So Idomeneus fled from Crete to settle in Italy.

Ortygia: an earlier name for Delos.

Naxos: the island where Theseus deserted Ariadne after slaying the Minotaur in Crete. She was rescued by Bacchus, and therefore the island was sacred to him.

Donysa, Olearos, Paros: all islands of the group known as Cyclades.

Curetes: the name for the priests of Jupiter in Crete, where he was worshipped with noisy rites. He had been hidden on the island when a baby to escape being killed by his father, Cronos. His cries were covered up by the Curetes clashing their arms.

Pergamum: Virgil connects the historical town of Pergamum with Aeneas.

Dardanus and Iasius were brothers: Both married daughters of Teucer who was king in Asia Minor.

Corythus: an ancient town in Etruria, north of the Tiber river.

BRIGHT NOTES STUDY GUIDE

Ausonia: another name for Italy.

Dictaean: means Cretan from the name of the mountain, Dicte, in Crete.

Palinurus: the pilot.

Phineus: a king of Thrace whom the gods punished by sending the Harpies to destroy his house. But two of the famous Argonauts (sailors of the ship Argo who went in search of the golden fleece), Zetes and Calais, drove the Harpies off.

Stygian Waves: referring to the river Styx of the Underworld, where monsters lived.

Laomedon: organized the building of Troy, but refused to pay Apollo and Neptune for their work. The Harpy, Celaeno, is taunting the Trojans by reminding them that they are descended from a man famous for breaking his word.

Zacynthus, Dulichium: islands off the western coast of Greece.

Neritus: mountain of Ithaca.

Same: town on the island of Cephallenia.

Mt. Leucata: a mountain sacred to Apollo on the southern tip of the island of Leucadia.

Buthrotum: located in the region of Chaonia in northern Epirus.

(LINES 294-718.)

Having arrived at the city of Buthrotum, Aeneas heard the rumor that one of Priam's sons, Helenus, was the ruler. He had been captured in the Trojan war by Pyrrhus and after the latter's death received a portion of the kingdom and Andromache (first married to Hector, and then to her captor, Pyrrhus) as wife. Sure enough, the first person Aeneas met was Andromache weeping by the river Simois (named after the Trojan River). She told him all that had happened to her since her capture by Pyrrhus. At this point, Helenus himself came out of the city, thrilled to find some fellow Trojans. Aeneas, after a few days rest, decided to go to Helenus (he possessed prophetic powers) and find out if he knew the will of Apollo and if he could advise him how to avoid more misfortunes. Helenus gave a lengthy answer. He told Aeneas that though Italy seemed very close a long journey was still ahead of him, for the western coast of Italy was his destination. To get there he would have to face the two perils of Scylla and Charybdis. These monsters guarded the Strait of Messina between Italy and Sicily. Scylla had six heads with which she snatched men from unsuspecting ships which came too close to the Italian shore. Charybdis was whirlpool on the Sicilian side which sucked the ships down as they tried to escape from Scylla. Therefore, though it was much shorter to go through the strait, Helenus advised Aeneas to go the long way around the southern coast of Sicily. Above all, he must remember to reverence Juno and perform all the proper ritual to keep her favor. When they reached Cumae (near Naples) they were to seek counsel from the Sibyl there. She would tell them what the future would bring. When Helenus had given his advice he heaped gifts on the travelers, while Andromache gave a scarf of her own to Aeneas' son.

Everything went well as they crossed the small body of water between Epirus and Italy, and on sighting this longed-for country, Anchises filled a huge bowl with wine. Raising it on high to the gods, he prayed for their continued favor. They made a short stop to sacrifice to Juno, as they had been warned, but the sight of white horses on the hillside appeared as an omen of war. So they set sail again. They come to the fateful whirlpool of Charybdis and just barely managed to avoid it.

But a new danger faced them, for they beached their ships on the coast of Sicily which was the home of the Cyclops, huge one-eyed giants. Over the whole region towered the mighty volcano, Aetna. After hiding in the woods all night, they were startled by the grotesque figure of a young man, all in tatters and wild-looking, who rushed toward them. Grovelling piteously he begged them to take him along. He, Achaemenides, was one of Ulysses' companions, who had been left behind when Ulysses made his escape from the Cyclops, Polyphemus. For three months he had been living off berries and roots. Even if they were to kill him, it would still be better than being eaten by a Cyclops. As he spoke, Polyphemus appeared in the distance. Even though he could not see the Trojans on the shore (Ulysses had put out his one eye) he heard the noise of the oars in the water. He headed for the sound and waded far out into the sea. The fleet had gotten just out of reach. Polyphemus let out a roar of anger which summoned all the other Cyclops to the shore. They towered raging at the waters edge while the Trojans threw on all sail.

This was their last adventure till they got to Drepanum on the western tip of Sicily because Achaemenides was able to give them helpful information about the Sicilian coast. But Aeneas was not to leave Drepanum without suffering another sorrow - the loss of his father - for which he was completely unprepared. It was after leaving Drepanum that the storm arose (the point at which Virgil begins the tale in Book I) which drove them to the shores of Carthage. Aeneas finishes his story at last; the banquet is over.

Comment

In spite of the number of events in this passage, the reader still does not get the impression that Aeneas has really been through very much. The most important fact is the warning about Juno, which reminds us that it was Juno's anger in Book I which caused the storm to drive Aeneas off his course. But Juno could not for a long time bring herself to be friendly to Aeneas, and not yet could he found Rome.

NAMES AND PLACES

Hermione: the only child of Menelaus, king of Sparta (Lacedaemon), and Helen (daughter of Leda and Jupiter). She had been promised to Orestes, son of Agamemnon and Clytemnestra. But when Clytemnestra had murdered her husband when he returned from Troy, Orestes had taken revenge by killing the murderess. For this crime of matricide the Furies drove Orestes mad. (See Aeschylus, Oresteia.)

Clarian: adjective from Claros referring to Apollo, because at Claros in Asia Minor there was a temple and an oracle dedicated to Apollo. The laurel was a bush sacred to the god and his priestess sat on the tripod when the oracle was consulted.

Circe: a sorceress who changed her guests into beasts, but from whom Ulysses managed to escape, fled from her island Aea, to a promontory off the coast of Latium.

Lakes: the marshy area round Avernus in Southern Italy was thought to be an entrance into the Lower World.

Locrians: colonizers of Southern Italy from Narycium on the mainland of Greece opposite Euboea. According to legend they were driven by storms to south Italy after the Trojan war. The historical fact is that all of southern Italy along the coast was settled in the ninth, eighth, and seventh centuries by Greeks. The area was known as Magna Graecia.

Lyctus: a city in Crete.

Sallentini: a people inhabiting the southernmost tip of Italy.

Philoctetes: a Greek hero from Meliboea in Thessaly who took part in the Trojan war. His claim to fame was killing Paris.

Petelia: another city in southern Italy, said to have been founded by Philoctetes.

Pelorus: northeastern promontory of Sicily on the strait of Messina.

Pachynus: southernmost point of Sicily.

Sibyl: a prophetess whose utterances were written on palm leaves. Aeneas is warned by Helenus not to let any breeze scatter the leaves, for then the prophecy would be unreadable.

Dodona: the location of most ancient of all the oracles of Greece, in Epirus.

Minerva's Height: a hill at the tip of the "heel" of Italy. The modern name is Castro.

Lacinium: a headland on the east coast of Bruttium on which was a temple of Juno.

Caulon and Scylaceum were cities further along the coast of Italy.

Enceladus: one of the giants who fought against the gods.

Sicanian Bay: the bay of Syracuse.

Alpheus: the god of the river of the same name in Greece which flows into the Ionian Sea near Olympia. He was pursuing the nymph, Arethusa, and Diana, to save her, changed her into a fountain on the island of Ortygia in the Syracusan harbor. The river-god still chased her under the sea to Ortygia, trying to mingle his stream with her waters.

Camerina: a Sicilian city which had been warned by an oracle never to drain the marsh nearby. When the inhabitants disobeyed, the enemy entering by the drained marsh was able to capture the town. All the proper names in this final section of the book are cities in Sicily. Near two of them, Drepanum and Lilybaeum, famous battles in the First Punic War took place. (Rome against Carthage 260-256 B. C.)

SUMMARY

The tale of Aeneas' travels, after the excitement of the fall of Troy is something of a disappointment to the reader. The book is full of names, places and events, similar to those in Homer's *Odyssey*, but it lacks the vigorous flavor of adventure. This is partly due to the fact that oracles always announce what is going to happen ahead of time, so that there is little sense of

BRIGHT NOTES STUDY GUIDE

suspense. It is also due to the fact that the gods are removed from any direct action. True, Aeneas consults Apollo's oracle, and sacrifices to Jupiter and Juno, but these gods do not themselves have anything to do with what happens. The apparent function of telling how Aeneas got from Troy to Carthage is the least important reason for the book. Virgil is really more concerned with unhappy recollections of the past (in the persons of Polydorus or Andromache, for instance) and the revelations concerning the future, which take place one after the other, rather than with the adventures themselves. But disappointing as the book is in many ways, it is still necessary in that it shows how much of a Trojan Aeneas still is, and how much a part of the Homeric tradition the *Aeneid* is.

THE AENEID

BOOK IV

. . . .

(LINES 1-197.)

We are now back to where we were in Book I, and queen Dido is suffering as only these wounded by love can suffer. After tossing and turning all night, going over and over in her mind Aeneas' words and remembering his every look and gesture, she runs to her sister, Anna, for counsel. To Anna Dido confesses that if she had not made up her mind to remain loyal to her long dead husband, Sychaeus, she would be more than willing to yield to this intense emotion she now feels. She had truly loved Sychaeus and now she recognizes an awakening of those long dead feelings. No, she will never break her former vows. But as she utters these noble words she bursts into tears on Anna's shoulder. Anna, wanting her sister's happiness and also the welfare of Carthage, says that she thinks Dido has remained a widow long enough. Reminding Dido of the numerous enemies around Carthage, she subtly suggests that marriage with Aeneas would bring glory to the city.

They decide to sacrifice to all the gods who might make such a happy event take place. Ceres, Apollo, and Bacchus are each given a sheep because they are connected with marriage rites. But to Juno, the guardian of women, whose special concerns were wedlock and childbirth, Dido sacrifices a pure white heifer. Radiantly beautiful, the queen performs all the necessary ritual of examining the entrails of the victims, as each day she goes through the same ceremonies. But ceremonies to the gods have no meaning for a woman whose whole being is focused on the love of a man. "Dido burns," are the words of Virgil. She wanders around the city in a fog of unreality. She is like a deer which wanders through the woods, crazed by the pain of an arrow firmly stuck in her side.

As an excuse to be with Aeneas she takes him on sightseeing tours of the city. Every time she begins to say something, however, the words choke in her throat. Every night they dine together and, unable to make conversation, she makes him repeat the same story of his adventures over and over again. Then, when everyone is gone, she is again left alone with the unending thoughts and wishes going round and round in her head. In her mind's eye she sees him beside her; oh, so clearly. She even tries the ruse of making his son, Ascanius, fond of her so that Aeneas may take notice. The queen, in her anguish, forgets the city entirely. All the buildings to be constructed, the military training of the young men, every scheme for the beautifying and strengthening of Carthage is abandoned.

It isn't long before Juno becomes aware of the consuming passion of her beloved Dido. She goes to Venus, since it was the latter who started the whole affair (see the end of Book I) and proposes marriage as the only fair solution. Carthage and its inhabitants would be Dido's dowry. But Venus isn't so easily fooled. Knowing that Juno wants to keep Aeneas from reaching Italy, she says she really does not know what is best to do, and maybe Jupiter should be consulted. Juno then unfolds her plan that the two should go hunting. In the middle of the hunt she will cause a storm and, when Dido and Aeneas come to a cave for shelter, she, Juno, will join them in wedlock. Venus finally consents.

At the crack of dawn the next day the gay hunting party sets out. What a procession! Prancing horses, hunting dogs, spears with points sparkling in the sunlight, and lastly the lovely queen, splendid in purple, carrying a gold quiver, all process out of the gates. But as beautiful as Dido is, just as beautiful is Aeneas. The only being he can be compared to is the god, Apollo, when he sets out from his winter home to visit the island of Delos. Even young Ascanius has a horse and gallops about, hoping to get a boar at least. But the hunt is not long in progress when the storm, contrived by Juno, breaks. The rain and hail scatters the group all over the place, and "Dido and the Trojan leader arrive at the same cave." The only attendants at this wedding are the forces of nature. For marriage torches there is only lightning. For the wedding hymn there is the wailing of wood-nymphs (for thus Dido thinks of the moaning of the storm-tossed trees). In her mind she sees Juno and mother Earth as divine witnesses of the long desired event. To Dido it is a wedding, but to the outside world it is a sin. The evil goddess, Rumor, takes care of that. Nothing in the world travels as fast as Rumor with her countless eyes, ears and never silent mouths. Her power is so great that she can strike terror into mighty cities. Sometimes her words are true, but just as often, they are false. Now gleefully she spreads the gossip: Dido and Aeneas are lovers!

Comment

In this passage events move quickly, and all too realistically to their unavoidable conclusion. The feeling of tragedy, which increases as the story progresses, is present even in the opening lines of the book. With what skill Virgil accomplishes this! He portrays Dido not as a wicked woman of passion, but as a radiantly beautiful queen who falls in love because of her longing for heroic greatness. The nobility of Aeneas touches a responsive chord in her soul. Yet how clearly we see the power of love in the **simile** of the wounded deer. The very words Virgil uses show that the two were destined for this tragic love. For when he describes Aeneas, he compares him to Apollo in the same manner that he had compared Dido to Apollo's twin sister, Diana, in Book I. The adjective, pulcherrimus, (meaning extraordinarily beautiful) is used in the masculine form for Aeneas, and in its feminine form for Dido. We tend to shy away from using the word, beautiful, for a man. To the Greeks and Romans, however, it had no bad association. In telling what happened in the cave, Virgil shows tremendous insight and understanding. It affected Aeneas very little; so he is barely mentioned. It was not a formal wedding, but Dido's believing that it was and her wanting it to be so gave it a reality for her. At such times a woman always believes that the presence of the divine has sanctified her actions. The last dramatic image in the passage is that of exulting Rumor. This too, is so true of life. Almost before the deed occurs, everyone knows about it. Slowly the tragedy deepens.

NAMES AND PLACES

Erebus: a lesser divinity, whose name signifies darkness and is therefore applied to the gloomy area through which the shades must pass on their way to the underworld.

Iarbas: the king of Gaetulia which boarded on Dido's Carthage. He had sought her hand in marriage but was refused.

Syrtes: two gulfs on the eastern half of the north African coast. They were unfriendly due to their quicksands and exposure to the north winds, the rocky shore, and variable tides.

Barcaeans: wild tribes of the desert of North Africa.

Lyaeus: another name for Bacchus.

Massylians: a North African tribe from the area west of Carthage.

Lycia: district on the southwest of Asia Minor.

Dryopes: a people living in Asia Minor.

Agathyrsi: tribe from Sarmatia on the Danube. The various names of these tribes are used to show that peoples from the ends of the earth worshipped Apollo.

Juno And Mother Earth: represent gods of sky and earth. Here they perform the function of taking the auspices, a ceremony which proceeded a wedding. Juno also acts as the pronuba, the matron who conducted the bride to the bridal room.

Coeus And Enceladus: giants, known as Titans, who scaled Mt. Olympus. They were sons of Mother Earth. When one brood of Titans, represented by Coeus, was hurled down from the mountain, Earth, in anger, produced another crop, of whom Enceladus was one.

(LINES 198-449.)

When the story reaches Iarbas, Dido's rejected suitor, he becomes thoroughly upset. Raising his hands to his father, Jupiter Ammon, he complains that he has been dreadfully misused. It was he who gave Dido the parcel of ground on which to settle, and yet she could spurn him and then open her arms to Aeneas. What sort of justice was this? Jupiter is moved and sends Mercury to do something about the situation. After all, Aeneas was not saved from burning Troy for the arms of a woman. So Mercury is to remind Aeneas of his destiny and tell him to sail at once. And what does he find the great hero doing, but building palaces and temples for Carthage. The god reproaches him for being under Dido's thumb and forgetting his own glorious future. Even if the promise of his own kingdom in Italy does not move him, at least he should remember his son's future. Aeneas quickly comes to himself, but is now faced with the awful predicament: how to tell Dido. One plan after the next occurs to him, but none of them are any good. Finally he tells his men to ready the fleet, using utmost secrecy. When Dido seems to be in the right mood, he will tell her.

But women in love are not so easily deceived. The preparations for sailing do not escape her. Like a drunken Maenad in the orgies of Bacchus she accosts Aeneas with the age-old words of reproach: how will she live, what will she do, what of the enemies on all sides, her brother Pygmalion who murdered her father, or the furious rejected king, Iarbas? What has she done to be so treated? As a last ruse she suggests the possibility that she is carrying his child.

Aeneas is moved to terrible anguish with compassion for Dido and her grief but he has no alternative. He did not seek her, but she went after him. His love for the gods, for his father, for his son, must come first. Her complaining only makes things worse for both of them. "Not of my own free will do I pursue Italy."

Needless to say, these words are small comfort. A tirade of despair pours forth from her lips: he is not the son of a goddess, but the son of hard granite. She welcomed him when a beggar thrown on the shores by the storms.

Now she has become the beggar. He will rue the day, however, for she will haunt him wherever he goes. Even when she is dead, her ghost will never leave him. In utter agony she breaks off the flow of words and flees to her bed. Aeneas goes to look after the preparations for departure, sorrowful but determined. The men are eagerly at work, like ants. (A wonderful **simile** of the busy, tireless work of ants, follows). Slowly but surely all Dido's regal pride and self-respect leave her as she sees this energy which promises that Aeneas is going. Again and again she tries to get him to change his mind. Finally she goes to her sister to beg her to use her influence with him. If Anna could at least persuade him not to leave till the more favorable spring weather comes, she would be satisfied. But Anna's words can not move the heroic greatness of Aeneas, anymore than the strong north winds, with all their buffeting, can uproot a mighty oak tree. Still the hero has human qualities for, in spite of all, the scene, which could end with him appearing so cruel, ends with him weeping also.

Comment

This passage is important for the understanding of the character of both Dido and Aeneas. Dido, in breaking her vows to her dead husband, lost her self-respect. When her love, which was the reason for breaking the vows in the first place, is treated as worthless her only choice is death. Several times she hints at this death, the final time being in her speech to Anna. Her self-respect is the core of her nature and this is what makes her tragedy so great. As for Aeneas, we see both his humanity and his heroic greatness, if we read with understanding. He is no heartless cad, as we might think at first glance. For one brief moment he was happy, caught up in the affairs of the present and free of the burdens of past (Troy) and future (Rome). But men with a destiny seem not to be allowed happiness. The true importance of the oak tree **simile** is its emphasis on suffering, for Aeneas suffers in having to leave Dido. With reason does Virgil use the adjective pius to describe the hero as he determines to go. His sense of duty to gods and ancestors and descendants (all this is implied in the word pius) is what gives him the strength to carry out his resolution. His heart may be divided, but his duty is plain. In that is Aeneas' tragedy.

NAMES AND PLACES

Ammon: god of the Egyptian city of Thebes. The Romans later identified him with Jupiter. He was the father of Iarbas by a Libyan (Garamantean) nymph.

Paris: Iarbas, in contempt, compares Aeneas to Paris because he is the successful suitor of another man's wife.

Maeonian: north-eastern portion of Lydia, bordering on Phrygia. Here Virgil thinks of it as Phrygian.

Cyllenius: a name for Mercury because he was born on Mt. Cyllene in Arcadia. His mother, Maia, was the daughter of Atlas. Virgil personifies the mountain, Atlas, which marked the western limit of the known world to the ancients.

Elissa: another name for Dido.

Hyrcania: a province in Persia along the south-eastern shore of the Caspian Sea.

Anchises: there was a legend that Diomedes stole the ashes of Anchises but later restored them to Aeneas.

Thyiads: Attic women (from near Athens) who worshipped Bacchus on Mt. Parnassus in Thebes in wild rites. The orgies were accompanied by waving a wand (the thyrsus) twined with ivy and topped by a pine cone, and clashing cymbals. Music was furnished by a flute-like instrument.

(LINES 450-705.)

When there is no possible hope, Dido seeks death. As omens of this sad end she sees the holy water on the altars grow dark and the wine poured out to the god become blood. She tells no one of the dreadful sign. A second portent is the sound of her dead husband's voice coming from the marble chapel she had dedicated to him. Even the owl, screeching at night seems to foretell evil. Every night she dreams that Aeneas is haunting her, hounding her, the way the Furies hounded Orestes. Slowly the scheme for death evolves in her mind. Going to Anna, she tells her that she has decided to use the forces of magic to rid herself of this all-consuming love. A priestess from Ethiopia is to help her. She wants Anna to have a huge pyre built and to place on it the bed that she and Aeneas had shared, and the armor and clothes he had left behind. Anna suspects nothing and carries out her sister's wishes. Dido herself checks everything and arranges Aeneas' possessions carefully on the bed. The priestess calls upon the gods of the magical number three, Hecate and

Diana, and the gods of the underworld, Erebus and Chaos. All the proper charms of love and sorcery are used: herbs cut in the moonlight with bronze sickles filled with black poison, and the forelock of a colt taken at birth. Dido herself stands at the altar wearing only one sandal and her clothes hanging down unbelted. Everything is set for the ceremony next day.

Night comes, but it brings sleep neither to Dido nor to Aeneas. Round and round go the thoughts in the head of the tortured queen of Carthage. Perhaps she should marry one of the Numidian princes, or maybe she could follow the Trojan ships to Italy; but they would never welcome her. If only she had never become involved with such a passion in the first place. As she was tossing, racked by indecision, Aeneas was snatching his last night's rest on the poop deck. Naturally he dreams: a god, looking like Mercury, appears, and warns him to set sail instantly. Dido is planning to burn their ships before they can get away. Without wasting a moment Aeneas rouses all his men, gives the order to cut the cables, and they are away, churning up the waters. When Dido looks out from the watch-tower at the first streak of dawn, she sees the sails white and full in the distance. Cursing herself for her inability to have ordered the Trojans slain, her indecision when she could have set fire to Aeneas' camp, she calls upon the gods to hear her evil prophecy. Aeneas will come to an untimely death and lie unburied in the sand, and never, never will there be any possibility of friendship between the nation that he should found and her kingdom.

These words hurled at heaven bring an end to her irresolution. She tells her old nurse, Barce, to go and get Anna and to make sure that she is ritually cleansed for the ceremony of burning the great pyre. The nurse leaves Dido and she, made strong at last with her dreadful purpose, climbs the funeral pyre. Collapsing on the bridal bed she reviews the past and begs to be released from her woes. She has built the city of Carthage and thus avenged her husband's murder. All would have been well, and she would have been happy, if the Trojan ships had never been blown to her shores. "I have lived," she says, "and accomplished the course of life which fortune gave." Before any of the watchers realizes what is happening, she stabs herself and falls back in a faint. Loud wails fill the air. Anna comes running. Too late it dawns on her why the pyre was built. Scrambling up she tries frantically to stem the flow of blood, and her robe grows red. Three times Dido tries to rise up on her elbow. Finally she moans in pain, and Juno, pitying her, sends her messenger Iris (the rainbow goddess) to release the soul from the tortured body. Gently the goddess cuts a few golden hairs from the queen's head to symbolize her sacrifice to the gods of the underworld. Dido breathes her last.

Comment

This passage is filled with the presence of death, although Dido puts it off as long as she possibly can. The longer she delays, however, the more degraded she becomes. Her inner knowledge of this degradation increases the tragedy. But when she finally steels herself to the inevitable deed, once more she becomes a majestic queen and returns to the greatness she had when we first met her in Book I, dispensing justice before the temple of Juno. Through death, the poet defeats passion, while Aeneas, with still another sorrow added to his burden, sails on to fulfill his destiny.

NAMES AND PLACES

Pentheus: a king of Thebes who hid himself so that he could watch the mysteries of Bacchus. He was discovered, and torn to pieces. His madness caused him to see everything double.

Erebus And Chaos: gods of the underworld especially associated with magic.

Hecate: she was associated with the moon, in the heavens, with Diana on earth, and with Persephone (the queen of the underworld) under the earth. Thus she was thought to have three heads, that of a horse, a dog, and a lion. She was worshipped at places where three roads met, and came to be regarded as the goddess of witchcraft. The passage which follows is full of magical lore which had a long literary tradition.

Tithonus: brother of Priam who received the gift of immortality from the gods, due to the prayers of Aurora, goddess of the Dawn. But he was not given eternal youth, and eventually shriveled up with old age. In pity, Aurora changed him to a grasshopper.

unburied: Aeneas reigned only three years and his body was swept away by the river Numicus. The rest of her curse involves the adventures of Aeneas in Books VII-XII, with a reference to the Punic wars. The "avenger" is meant to be Hannibal, the famous Carthaginian general.

Proserpina: (Greek name was Persephone) Pluto's queen in the underworld was supposed to cut the thread of life of women. The lock of hair refers to the custom of taking a few hairs from a victim before it was sacrificed. The dying were considered offerings to the gods of the underworld, and a similar rite was usually performed.

Dis: another name for Pluto.

SUMMARY

Book I opened with a storm of nature, symbolizing the many storms in Rome's future, eventually subdued by Augustus. Book IV, showing poetic continuity, concerns the storm of man's greatest emotion, love. In this book Virgil is perhaps farthest from Homer. The **theme** of men attracted to women is barely suggested in Homer. Hector bids a touching farewell to Andromache. Achilles sulks because Agamemnon stole his captive princess. Odysseus leaves Calypso, Circe, and Nausicaa, but no tragedy is involved. It is Virgil who has the "humanity" to elevate the deserted woman to the position of a heroine of tragedy. His conception of love as a tragic force is what makes him a timeless poet, with appeal even in this modern day. We see the suffering of Dido torn between the desires of the heart and the need for self respect and greatness. We see Aeneas facing the forces of passion, bearing their pain, and finally conquering them. Throughout the book runs the **theme** of the double conflict: the historical one between Rome and Carthage, hinted at in Book I in the opposing goddesses, Venus and Juno; and the human one. In the sense that Book IV stresses the struggle between personal happiness and heroic glory, between passion and control, it can be thought of as the **climax** of the whole poem.

THE AENEID

The flames of Dido's funeral pyre cause a glow to spread over the sky which the fleeing Trojans cannot help but see. Everyone is filled with a sense of doom. To increase their downcast spirits a storm comes up and the chief helmsman, Palinurus, is not able to hold the course for Italy. The head winds are too strong. He advises Aeneas, however, that they can bear off and make for Sicily which is not too far distant. Aeneas gives his assent since the change of plan will enable him to visit his old friend Acestes. In addition, his father had died on Sicilian shores, so the island is doubly dear to him. Acestes, having seen the ships in the distance, is down on the shore to welcome the travelers when they land. The next morning Aeneas announces to everyone that it was a year ago that his father, Anchises, died. In his honor, he has decided to set the day apart for sacrificing and feasting. He also tells them that in nine days he will set up a great field day for sports. As he speaks, a snake slithers from behind the altar, winds its way among the sacrificial foods, tastes them, and disappears without hurting anyone. Holding it as a good omen, Aeneas finishes the sacrifice of two sheep, two pigs, and two heifers. Nine days later the sun rises in a cloudless sky and the Trojans and Sicilians gather together to take part in the sports.

The first contest is a boat race which turns out to be dreadfully tense. The captain of one boat, Gyas, pushes his helmsman, Menoetes, into the water for failing to carry out an order. While Gyas is taking over the helm, the other ships pass him. Sergestus is now in the lead but, rounding the mark (a rock which stuck out above the water) too close, his ship runs aground on a hidden ledge and all the oars on the port side are broken. Mnestheus, having prayed earnestly to Neptune, gleefully overtakes the foundering vessel. With only one more to pass he is certain of victory. The bows of the two ships are just about even, and it is Cloanthus' turn to pray. (He is the captain of the fourth vessel.) He promises a white bull to the sea nymphs, the Nereids, if they will help him. (For some reason they seem to have more power at this point than Neptune!) Cloanthus pulls ahead and is proclaimed victor. Crowned with a green garland of bay leaves he receives his prize, a cloak of purple embroidered with gold. The other three captains get prizes too, so no one's feelings are hurt.

Comment

Virgil is following Homeric tradition in his "field day" in Book V. In Homer there are funeral games in honor of Patroclus (*Iliad* XXIII, 262 f.). However, the boat race is original with Virgil, as is the later riding exhibition. All the sports have one thing in common: the man least expected to win, wins!

NAMES AND PLACES

Eryx: son of Neptune and Venus; thus half-brother of Aeneas. He was king in Sicily.

Acestes: Since Laomedon had refused to pay Neptune his wages for building Troy, the god sent a great sea-monster to which maidens were to be thrown as prey. One clever father sent his daughter, Segesta, to Sicily to avoid this doom. Acestes was her son.

snake: thought of as the guardian spirit of tombs. His seven coils stress the magic number seven.

Phaethon: son of the Sun-god. He begged his father to let him drive the chariot of the Sun, and going too close to the earth in North Africa began to burn everything. In the passage, Virgil is using the name of the son to mean Apollo for poetic effect. A thunderbolt hurled Phaethon to earth and restored the sun.

Mnestheus, Sergestus, Cloanthus: Prominent Roman families of Virgil's time liked to think of themselves as having Trojan ancestors; the Memmians from Mnestheus, the Sergians from Sergestus, the Cluentians from Cloanthus.

Phorcus: a son of Neptune and father of frightful beasts who had hissing serpents for hair, claws of brass, wings, and enormous teeth. They were called Gorgons.

Panopea: a sea nymph.

Portunus: an Italian god of the harbors.

Meliboea: town in Thessaly famous for its purple dye.

(LINES 286-603.)

Now follow three traditional sports: racing, boxing, and archery. The foot race is exciting because two very close friends take part, Nisus and Euryalus. Nisus is far ahead when he slips on a spot where the heifers had been killed for the sacrifice. But though he can not get up in time to keep the first place, he thinks of his friend who is third and manages to trip up the number two man, Salius. Euryalus wins, but Salius of course is mad at the foul play. To calm everyone, Aeneas gives him a lion's hide as a prize. Even Nisus gets a trophy, since Fortune was responsible for his fall. So he receives a shield Aeneas had captured from a Greek seven years before. The first prize, a horse with all its trappings, seems hardly interesting at all.

The boxing match takes place between a Trojan super-man, Dares, and the Sicilian champion, Entellus. In fact, Dares is so powerful looking that at first no one from the Sicilian ranks will fight with him. Entellus gets up reluctantly only after much urging from Acestes. To make the match more equal, Aeneas provides them both with gloves of the same weight. It is Entellus, although he is much older, who delivers the final punches. Having fallen once when his opponent dodged a blow, he almost goes berserk in eagerness to finish Dares off. But Aeneas calls a halt. To show off his mighty strength Entellus takes his caestus (a thong loaded with lead and wound around the hand as a sort of boxing glove) and in front of the spectators, beats out the brains of the bull he had won with one blow. Dares staggers down to the water, coughing out blood and broken teeth.

The archery contest comes as pleasant relief. Aeneas has a mast brought from one of the ships and set up at a distance. A live dove is hung from the top as the mark. The first arrow, narrowly missing the terrified bird, sticks firm in the mast. The second man's arrow cuts the cord which ties the bird, and off she flies. In the nick of time, the third contestant takes aim and wings the dove. This leaves Acestes, who had decided to compete in spite of his years, with nothing to shoot. So he lets fly an arrow into the heavens. Catching fire it vanishes with a trail of flames behind it, like a shooting star. The crowd is struck dumb with amazement, and Aeneas interprets the marvel as a sign showing that Acestes is the winner. His trophy is a huge embossed bowl which had belonged to Aeneas' own father, Anchises.

The last scheduled event is a horse show, put on by young Ascanius and his friends. The boys, divided into three companies of twelve each, file down the center of the arena, then wheel. Half the group goes one way, and half the other. On each side there are three groups of six, and these charge each other across the open field. When they are just about to meet, the captains give a signal, and they wheel again, pretending to flee. Performing many other skillful maneuvres, the boys show off their horsemanship to the delight of their proud fathers. (Virgil is giving a mythological explanation for the Ludus Troiae, a sport revived by Augustus in his youth-fitness program.)

Comment

The descriptions of the various sports are really quite vivid, though in some places they tend to be too long. The reader does wonder, however, where such an enormous number of prizes came from, especially if he knows anything about the tiny size of ancient ships! But it is important to notice the change that has taken place in Aeneas. He is the on-looker, the director, much more than the participant. Virgil calls him "father Aeneas" (pater), much more than he calls him "noble Aeneas" (pius).

NAMES AND PLACES

Olive crowns: the traditional prizes given at the Olympic games in Greece.

Thracians And Amazons: were noted for their skill in archery.

shield: the trophy given to Salius had belonged to a Greek who had dedicated it to Neptune, and then taken it from the temple when he went to war.

Paris: more famous as a prize-fighter than a warrior

Amycus: son of Neptune, king of the Bebryces (a mythical people in Bithynia) had world-wide renown as a boxer.

Hercules: the most famous of mythological heroes, known especially for performing twelve impossible labors. He also boxed with Eryx (see above) and killed him. His grandfather was Alcaeus, from whom came the name Alcides.

Erymanthus: mountain in Arcadia in Greece where the famous boar, which Hercules killed, lived.

Cisseus: king of Thrace, father of Hecuba, Priam's wife.

Labyrinth: according to legend, a winding maze of paths in Crete at the end of which was the half-bull, half-man beast kept by Minos the king of Crete. Modern excavation has uncovered a huge palace at Knossos with innumerable rooms and halls from which the ancient legend may have had its start.

Carpathian Sea: between Crete and the island of Rhodes.

(LINES 604-871.)

All of a sudden the happy events of the field day are interrupted by horrible news. The ships, hauled up on the beach, are burning. Not only that but the women, the very wives of the men participating in the sports, start the fire. Of course, it isn't completely their fault. Juno, the ever present enemy of the Trojans, is the source of the dreadful crime. She had sent her messenger, Iris, down to the women as they sat discontented by the deserted ships. Iris disguises herself as one of the Trojan women and runs around spreading more dissatisfaction. For seven years they have been chasing a fleeing Italy. Why shouldn't they settle down and build a new Troy right where they are? If the ships are destroyed, they will have to stay in Sicily; now is the time for action. She picks up a burning stick from the fire at the altar of Neptune, and throws it at one of the ships with all her strength. The women are taken completely by surprise. One of them points out to her friends that she who spoke is not the person she looks like. She is far too beautiful; she does not walk as a mortal walks. The goddess vanishes leaving a rainbow in the sky and all the women in a frenzy hurl sticks from the fire at the ships.

Ascanius, still in his mock armor, gallops down to the water's edge, followed by Aeneas and the crowd. Too late the women realize what they have done. Not all the water that the Trojans pour on has any effect on the fury of the blaze. Tearing his clothes in despair, pius Aeneas calls on Jupiter to save them, or else kill him then and there with his thunderbolt. Almost before the words are out of his mouth, a downpour comes. The half-burnt timbers are drenched and all but four boats are saved from the disaster. Up to now, Aeneas himself has not completely made up his mind what to do. He too, has been torn between Sicily and Italy. Now wise old Nautes comes to the hero with the suggestion that they leave all the unadventurous people who are too worn out to go any further, and go on to Italy without them. Those left behind can found their own city in Sicily.

That night, as Aeneas is weighing the pros and cons, his dead father appears in a vision. He tells Aeneas to follow the advice of Nautes and when he gets to the Italian shore near Avernus (where the ancients believed there was an entrance to the underworld) he was to let the Sibyl lead him to the lower regions where he, Anchises, would be waiting for him. There he would see the future revealed to him. So the next day everyone joins in marking out the site for the new Sicilian city of Acesta. After nine days of feasting and sacrificing, the time for sad farewells is at hand. Those who chose to stay behind watch the oars of the ships they might have been on, as the fleet pulls off into the distance.

Meanwhile Venus, on her guard because of Juno's latest trick, goes to Neptune to get a guarantee from him that nothing will go wrong this time. The king of the seas tells her she need not be afraid for her son any more. Only one man will die before the Trojans reach Avernus. Having said these words, he rides over the ocean, calming the heavy surf. Aeneas gives the order to crowd on sail and Palinurus sets the course for Italy. Poor Palinurus! Though he was completely innocent of any wrong to the gods or to his friends, Neptune had set his eye on him. Disguising himself as one of the Trojans, he approaches the steersman and offers to relieve him at the helm. But Palinurus, loyal to Aeneas as always, refuses. The god has not other choice but to make him fall asleep. Moments later he falls overboard. In spite of this calamity the ship seems to keep on her course for a few more hours as they make for the bay of Cumae (near modern Naples). When Aeneas finally realizes that the ship is drifting aimlessly he takes over the helm himself, stunned by his friend's loss.

Comment

In this passage, Aeneas, after one last moment of irresolution, turns decisively to his destined task. Although it had been made quite clear in Book III by Helenus that his new home was to be Italy, Aeneas kept wanting to take the easier path. First it was Carthage; then it was Sicily, but always at the moment of greatest trial one of the gods comes to his aid, either by jogging his memory, or else by enlisting the forces of nature on his side.

NAMES AND PLACES

Doryclus: brother of Pheneus, king of Thrace.

Rhoeteum: a rocky strip of coast along the Hellespont.

Vulcan: god of Fire.

Nautes: beloved of Minerva because he brought the tiny wooden statue of the goddess, the Palladium, with him from Troy. The Nautii, a prominent family during the days of the early Republic, claimed descent from him.

Elysium: according to Virgil, the portion of the lower world where the heroes went after death. Tartarus is sometimes used to mean the whole of the lower world, but here the reference is more probably to the section where bad heroes lived in constant torture.

Idalium: town in Cyprus sacred to Venus.

Laurentum: an ancient town in Latium near the Tiber river.

Peleus: king of the Myrmidons in Phthia in Thessaly, father of Achilles. The reference is to Neptune's rescue of Aeneas when Achilles was after him, as told by Homer in the *Iliad*, XX: 79-352.

Glaucus: a lesser sea-divinity, overgrown with shellfish and seaweed.

Palaemon: son of Ino who was driven mad by Juno. She threw herself and her son into the sea, and they were changed into sea-gods.

Phorcus: another sea-god, sometimes called the "old man of the sea" by Homer. (see earlier note in the chapter).

Thetis: mother of Achilles. The rest of the names are sea-nymphs daughters of Nereus, as was Thetis herself.

Lethe: the river of forgetfulness in the underworld. The souls of the dead drank of its water before they returned to the world to inhabit new bodies and forgot their former life as mortals completely.

Sirens: beautiful sea-nymphs who enticed sailors to destruction on their rocks by their lovely songs. Virgil locates them near the bay of Naples. After Ulysses tricked them, they drowned themselves. (*Odyssey* XII: 178-200.)

SUMMARY

Although at times the reader feels that Virgil leans a little heavily on Homeric tradition when he inserted the descriptions of the funeral games, most of them are tense little dramas on their own. This is especially true of the boat race. The whole book is necessary for understanding the growth of Aeneas' character. It also shows Virgil's belief that the divine plays a crucial role in man's life.

THE AENEID

BOOK VI

....

(LINES 1-235.)

At long last the Trojan exiles reach the shores of Italy. The eager adventurers leap ashore to explore, but Aeneas heads for the higher ground where there is the temple of Apollo. Nearby is the cave of the Sibyl who is Apollo's prophetess. On the gates of the temple are beautiful sculptures representing the legends of Crete. Aeneas and some of his friends stop to look at the gates, but are called away by the Sibyl who senses that the power of the god is going to come upon her. The Trojans must be ready to hear her prophecy. Suddenly she falls into a trance; her breath comes quickly; tremors shake her body. Her last coherent words are a command to Aeneas to make his prayer to Apollo before the moment passes. Aeneas prays for a revelation from the oracle and promises to build a temple of solid marble to the god and to establish a festival in his honor. The priestess sways more wildly, and then abruptly is still. From her lips comes the gloomy prophecy: for the Trojans more war, more bloodshed, and Juno's continued hatred, all because of another foreign bride (the first was Helen stolen by Paris). All these he must face more boldly than ever, and from a Greek city will come the first sign of safety.

Aeneas answers that after all he has been through, there is no form of struggle or danger he can not face. He begs her only to show him how to get to the underworld to see his father. She answers that it is quite easy to get down to the underworld, but very few manage to make it up again, unless they are under the special protection of Jupiter. First he must find the golden branch which Proserpina, the queen of the lower regions likes so much. If he finds it and can break it off easily, he will know fortune is with him. But he must bury the body of a friend who has died without his knowing it. Then he may try the road to the underworld.

Aeneas and his friend, Achates, leave the gloomy cave. Walking along the beach they are filled with dark thoughts. Suddenly they see a corpse on the ground in front of them. It is the bugler, Misenus, who drowned when they were seeking the oracle from the Sibyl. With many tears, Aeneas and his friends set to work to build the funeral pyre. All the while they are cutting down the trees Aeneas is praying in his heart for a sign of the golden branch. Then he sees two doves, the messengers of his mother, Venus, and is filled with joy. They lead him to the mouth of the cave of Avernus and suddenly settle on a tree. There the gold branch shone out, as yellow mistletoe does in winter. Effortlessly Aeneas breaks it off and carries it to the Sibyl. When the funeral pyre has burnt to the ground, the hero takes the urn with the ashes and buries it together with the dead man's armor, oar, and trumpet. Over everything he heaps a huge mound of earth. Only then is he free to make his way to the underworld.

Comment

This book starts out on a mysterious and awesome note with its use of the words "cave", "hidden", and "gloomy". It also has many divine revelations, the first of which occurs in this passage. Lastly, it is full of symbolism. The sculptures on the gate of Apollo's temple recall the murals on the temple of Juno in Carthage. And throughout the book there runs a deep religious undercurrent: Aeneas' prayer to Apollo, the Sibyl's prophecy, and the funeral of Misenus are but foretastes.

NAMES AND PLACES

Daedalus: the designer of the labyrinth, the den of the Minotaur, half-bull, half-man, for king Minos in Crete. When he incurred Minos' anger he fled from the island on wings which he had made and landed at Cumae.

Androgeos: son of Minos went to Athens to take part in the games in honor of Athena. When he had won every contest, the king of Athens, Aegeus, set him to fight the wild bull of Marathon, which killed him. In consequence Minos imposed a tribute from the Athenians of seven boys and seven girls to be sent every year for the Minotaur to eat. The son of the Athenian king, Theseus, finally brought an end to this tribute by killing the Minotaur. Ariadne, Minos' daughter helped him by giving him a ball of string which he unwound as he made his way into the labyrinth, and rewound to find his way out again. She went with the Athenians as they escaped from Crete, but was later abandoned on the way on the island of Naxos.

Pasiphae: wife of Minos, and also mother of the Minotaur.

Icarus: son of Daedalus who left Crete with his father. He flew too close to the sun so that the wax on his wings melted and he fell into the sea.

Cecrops: the mythical founder of Athens.

Trivia: a name for Diana because she was worshipped at the place where three roads (tres viae) crossed.

Aeacus: ancestor of Achilles. Apollo guided the arrow which Paris shot and by which Achilles died.

another Achilles: the king of the land Aeneas must conquer in Italy in order to found his city. His name is Turnus.

Graecian city: the city of Pallantium, ruled by Evander, who came from Greece. Aeneas goes to Evander for aid. Pallantium was on the Palatine hill, one of the seven hills of Rome.

Acheron: a river of the underworld whose overflow was thought to form Lake Avernus and the marshy region around it. Even today there are sulphuric fumes and other signs of volcanic action in this area.

Orpheus: a musician-poet of mythology who descended into the lower world to get back his wife Eurydice. He played so beautifully on his lyre that his wish was granted on condition that he not look back at her till they reached earth. At the last minute he turned around to make sure she was following, and so lost her forever.

Castor and Pollux: half-brothers who loved each other dearly. Their mother was Leda. Castor's father was Tyndareus, king of Sparta and father of Helen. Jupiter was the father of

Pollux, which made Pollux immortal. Both were conceived the same night and so were twins. When Castor was killed Pollux was desperate with grief. Finally Jupiter allowed the twins to take turns sharing life. Each spent one day in the underworld and the next day with the gods.

Theseus: went to the underworld to rescue Proserpina who had been carried off from her mother, Ceres, by the king of the lower regions, Pluto, whose other name was Dis.

Alcaeus: grandfather of Hercules whose last labor was to bring up from the underworld the three-headed dog, Cerberus.

Cocytus: one of the rivers that bounded the Lower World. It was the river of wailing and a tributary of the Acheron, river of woe.

Misenus: Virgil incorporates part of an early legend which dealt with the death of a comrade named Misenus. To this day a cape at one end of the bay of Naples bears his name.

(LINES 235-627.)

Into the dark, damp, smelly cave Aeneas goes. There he and the Sibyl perform ritual sacrifices to the gods of the lower regions. Then, as the sun rises, the earth rumbles with the threat of the volcano. The Sibyl shrieks at the Trojans to get out quickly. Aeneas she commands to unsheathe his sword and follow her. Down they go, through gloomy, ghostly passages. In front of the gates of the underworld they come upon Grief, Care, Disease, Old age, Fear, Famine, Poverty, Death, Misfortune, Sleep, Guilty Conscience, War, and Strife. They are enough to panic any man! Other monsters, Harpies and Gorgons seem to come at the hero, and he is about to slash at them with his sword but the Sibyl prevents him. They are only ghosts. They come to the bank of the river Acheron. Crowds of men and women, boys and girls are standing at the river's edge, begging the hideous ferryman, Charon, to take them across. Bewildered, Aeneas asks his guide what is happening. She tells him that all the people trying to get over the river are the unburied dead. Charon can not take them across until they have been given a proper funeral and their ashes are covered with earth. Only after they have wandered back and forth for a hundred years can Charon take them. Aeneas looks at them again with great pity. Going further, Aeneas finds several of his drowned companions and among them Palinurus, the faithful helmsman. He implores Aeneas to at least perform the ritual of throwing three handfuls of dirt on his corpse so that his spirit may have rest, or perhaps to take him back to the upper world. The Sibyl scolds him for trying to change the laws of heaven, but gives him one consolation. The people living along the coast near where his body was thought to have been washed up will build his tomb and name the promontory after him. They leave Palinurus a little cheered up and start to board Charon's boat. At first he refuses to take them, because earlier mortals whom he ferried over had all sorts of bad schemes up their sleeves. The Sibyl assures Charon that Aeneas is not going to carry off the underworld queen, as did Theseus, or do any other trick. As proof she holds out the golden branch which had been hidden under her robe. Charon is appeased, and ferries them over.

On the other side, the monster dog, Cerberus, snarls menacingly. To him the Sibyl throws a cake made of honey and sleep-inducing herbs. The dog promptly falls asleep and Aeneas enters the gate it had been guarding. The terrible wailing of new-born babies who died almost at birth, the moaning of suicides and unhappy lovers, meets their ears. It is here that

Aeneas comes upon angry Dido. He tries in vain to gain her understanding and forgiveness, for her grief is more than he can bear. His explanation that it was the decree of the gods which forced him to leave her fails completely to soften her anger. Keeping her eyes on the ground and without changing her expression at all, she walks away. The great hero can not keep back the tears.

On and on Aeneas and the Sibyl go through the half-light. Soon they find themselves surrounded by famous Trojan heroes who are delighted to see Aeneas and want to talk with him. Among then is the son of Priam, Deiphobus, whose body is so mutilated that Aeneas barely recognizes him. He tells the hero the story of his horrible death and Aeneas would have stayed with him longer, if the Sibyl had not reminded him that soon the time would be up. He must not forget that the main purpose of his coming was to see his father, Anchises. So they come to where the path divides. The right fork leads to the Elysian fields where they will find Anchises. The left leads to the dungeon of the damned with its massive gates. These souls must atone for the crimes they committed on earth. Rhadamanthus is their harsh judge. At each stroke of the whip which the goddess of vengeance, Tisiphone, wields a scream of anguish rends the air. Aeneas, with horrified fascination, looks back as he and the Sibyl set off on the path toward the Elysian fields. The Sibyl describes some of the punishments. The giant Tityos is condemned to having his liver forever eaten by a vulture. Ixion and Pirithous live under the constant threat of a rockslide from a mountain falling on them, while just beyond their reach is a table laden with delectable things to eat. (This punishment is usually assigned to Tantalus. Ixion's punishment is usually a fiery wheel and Pirithous is chained to a rock. Virgil changes the legend.) The Titans who tried to overthrow Jupiter are condemned to eternal torture. Phlegyas, who burned the temple of Apollo at

Delphi, speaks out his grim warning: "Learn justice, and do not despise the gods."

Comment

This long central section gives Virgil a chance for two things. 1.) He shows his tremendous knowledge of myths and superstition. Yet the stories of the heroes and heroines are carefully worked in to create an atmosphere of gloom and horror. The nobility and glory of Anchises' prophecy in the last section of the book is heightened by the tremendous contrast with the murky terror of the middle part. 2.) The poet puts a spotlight on the humanity and compassion of Aeneas. The meeting with Dido, and Deiphobus, the looking back are put in purposely to stress these qualities. For Virgil understanding the sufferings of others is part of the process of becoming a hero.

NAMES AND PLACES

Eumenides: a nice sounding name for the Furies, the goddesses of vengeance. It meant "well-wishers." The most famous were Tisiphone, Allecto (whom we meet in Book VII) and Megaera. Their mother was Night. Earth was Night's sister.

Stygian King: Pluto.

Phlegethon: river of fire in the underworld.

Centaurs: a wild race living on Mt. Pelion in Thessaly. They delighted in bull-killing, and according to most legends, were thought to be half man, half horse.

Briareus: a giant with a hundred hands.

Lerna: a marsh in southern Greece where the water-serpent, Hydra lived. She was killed by Hercules in the second of his twelve labors.

Chimaera: a fire-breathing monster with the head of a lion, the tail of a dragon, and a goat's body.

Geryon: a giant with three bodies, by slain Hercules.

Velia: a Greek town not far from modern Naples.

Pirithous: friend of Theseus, and originator of the idea of carrying off Proserpina.

Amphrysus: a river in Thessaly where Apollo tended the flocks of the king, Admetus.

Minos: king of Crete who became a judge in the underworld after his death. The other two judges were Rhadamanthus and Aeacus.

Phaedra: hanged herself because of her love for her stepson, Hippolytus.

Procris: checking up on her husband to see if he was faithful to her when he went hunting one day, was shot accidentally by one of his arrows.

Eriphyle: after being bribed to convince her husband, Amphiaraus, to war against Thebes, was slain by her son. The husband was killed in the war.

Evadne: jumped onto her husband's funeral pyre after he, like Amphiaraus, was killed in the war against Thebes.

Laodamia: killed herself when her husband was slain at Troy.

Caeneus: started out as a maiden, Caenis, but was changed into a boy by her lover Neptune. In the underworld she regained her feminine form.

Marpessa: a mountain in Paros, the island famous for marble. Dido is pale and unmoved, like marble.

Tydeus, Parthenopaeus, Adrastus: legendary heroes of the war of the Seven Against Thebes, the most important war before the expedition against Troy. The next group are heroes of the Trojan war.

Laconian Woman: Helen, who married Deiphobus after his brother Paris was killed.

Aeolus: (not the king of the winds) king of Thessaly, was not the father of Ulysses, to whom this passage refers. But it was said that his son, Sisyphus, was the father.

Aloeus: his wife, Iphimedia, and her lover, Neptune, had two sons, Otus and Ephialtes, who are generally called the sons of Aloeus. Their crime was trying to reach heaven by piling Ossa on Olympus, and Pelion on Ossa. (All three are mountains in Thessaly).

Salmoneus: king of Elis (southwestern Greece) who scornfully imitated the thunder and lightning of Zeus.

Lapiths: a tribe in Thessaly ruled by Pirithous, son of Ixion, whose bride was affronted by one of the Centaurs. Thus arose the famous struggle between the Lapiths and the Centaurs. (The most well-known portrayal of this battle was a frieze on the temple of Zeus at Olympia.

(LINES 628-901.)

At long last the gruesome journey nears its end. The hero and his aged guide reach the archway that opens onto the Elysian fields. At the entrance Aeneas sprinkles his body with water for purification, and plants the golden branch. Here is "the joyful land, the pleasant grassy spots, the happy abodes of the blessed groves." The atmosphere is purer, filled with a rosy glow. In such an enchanted place no one is miserable. Some take part in sports, other dance; Orpheus plays his lyre. The ancestors of the Trojans are there with their phantom horses and chariots. The good priests, the noblest poets, philosophers and scientists who have benefited mankind crowd around the two visitors from the upper world. The Sibyl asks the tall poet in the center of the group, Musaeus, (he was considered a father of poetry) where they can find Anchises. He shows them the way, over the ridge and down into the next valley. There Anchises is retelling the story of his race and their descendants. Tears spring to his eyes at the sight of his son as he runs toward him with outstretched arms. How long he has waited for him to come. Aeneas struggles vainly to embrace his father, but only clasps air. If he cannot touch him, at least he can ask questions. Seeing a large number of people clustered round the river Lethe in the distance, he asks who they are. They seem like a swarm of bees hovering around luscious white lilies in the summer. His father tells him that they are the lucky souls who are given a second chance at life. But first they must drink the waters of forgetfulness. Aeneas is filled with pity at the thought of so many souls longing for the light of earth again. Anchises realizes that his son does not fully understand and so gives him a lengthy explanation of the philosophy of the transmigration of souls. After men die, even those who are good, their souls are still contaminated by having been incased in mortal bodies. So in the underworld the soul must pay the penalty till the taint is washed away. At the end of the cycle of a thousand years, when the soul is completely pure again, it is ready to go back to earth and live in a new mortal body. The last thing they do is to drink of the river Lethe so that they will forget what their former life on earth was like.

At the end of this philosophic explanation Anchises leads his son to a rise of ground from which all the people waiting to go to earth can clearly be seen. Then, with ever mounting pride, he points out Aeneas' son, grandson, and descendants who will raise the glory of his line to the stars. Of those nearest in line to the front, the most famous is Romulus, who was to found Rome. Off to one side stands Numa, the second king of Rome, who was the author of her religious customs. Beyond him are the other kings, warring Tullus, boastful Ancus Marcius, and the three Etruscan kings, Tarquin, Servius Tullius, and Tarquin the Proud. The heroes of the early Republic come next: Brutus, who deposed the last king of Rome, Tarquin the Proud, and many others. Down the centuries Anchises traces the men who are to make Rome great. There are also the men responsible for the terrible years of civil war and among them Caesar and Pompey. In another group are those whose victories in war helped the spread of empire. With them are the great men who defeated the power of Carthage. But at the end of the line there stands a soul greater than all. He is Caesar Augustus. Under him the long lost Golden Age will return again to Italy. The wonderful order of his rule will extend even to the stars. There is virtually no end to the glorious array of Rome's heroes.

And the blessings Rome will give to mankind cannot be matched. Others may create more life-like sculpture, may be more clever orators, or wiser astronomers. "Your destiny, oh Roman, is to govern the peoples of the world with order, to plant in them the habit of peace, to spare the conquered, and to crush the proud."

But Anchises has not quite finished naming the souls when Aeneas sees a young man of great beauty with melancholy eyes, and wonders who he is. He is the young Marcellus whom Augustus adopted as his successor. All Rome loved him, but he died prematurely at the age of twenty. His great promise came to nothing. Never was there such a funeral, or such mourning. Anchises finishes speaking, and leads his son through the rest of the realm of the Elysian fields. Finally Aeneas takes his leave, his spirit fired with passion for renown. Through the gate of Sleep which was for false dreams, the hero and the prophetess make their way. Soon Aeneas is back with his friends. The sail north to Latium is short. "Anchors are cast from the bows; the sterns rest upon the shore."

Comment

This final section of Book VI resounds with the majesty of Rome's greatness. This is because the idea of the mission of Rome was almost a religion with Virgil. His creed is expressed in the stirring words toward the end of Anchises' speech: order, peace, mercy, justice, these were to be Rome's gifts to mankind. This magnificent revelation of Rome's destiny completely fills Aeneas. From this point on he consciously connects his mission with the future of Rome. The memory of his past fades before the hope of his future. The man has truly become the hero.

NAMES AND PLACES

Cyclops: one-eyed monsters who forged the iron for the walls of Pluto's palace.

Eridanus: the river Po flows underground for about two miles near its source which was why the ancients thought it rose in the underworld.

Titanian Star: sun. Many ancient philosophies (the most famous being the Stoic) held that the primary cause of life and motion was a sort of world-soul which had a nature like that of fire.

Procas, Capys, Numitor, Silvius Aeneas: traditional kings of Alba Longa.

Nomentum Etc.: old Latin towns near Rome.

Romulus: son of Ilia (Rhea Silvia, daughter of Numitor) and Mars. According to legend, he was the founder of Rome in 753 B.C.

Berecyntia: mountain in Phrygia sacred to Cybele, the Great Mother. She was represented as wearing a crown of towers.

Saturn: expelled from heaven by Jupiter, ruled Italy in the first Golden Age, when all was peace and happiness.

Garamantes: a tribe from the interior of Africa to which was sent an expedition in the time of Augustus.

Indus: here Virgil is referring to the east in general, by naming a prominent river there.

Maeotia: in southern Russia, area around the Sea of Azov.

Liber: the early Italian god of fertility, connected by the Romans with Bacchus. In the legend Bacchus' chariot, drawn by tigers, went as far as India. (Nysa is a mountain in the Punjab area of India.)

Cures: a town of the Sabines, birthplace of Numa Pompilius.

Fasces: rods (for whipping) and an axe which were carried in front of the highest officer as a symbol of power (imperium). At first they were the exclusive right of the kings, but after Brutus they were taken over by the consuls. When Brutus' sons conspired to restore the king to power, he put them to death.

Decii: three generations of this family fought for Rome in the battles with the Latins, Samnites, and Pyrrhus respectively. (The Latin war ended in 340 B.C., the Samnite in 290, and the war with Pyrrhus, from Epirus on the north-west coast of Greece, 280.)

Drusi: a good Roman family, but not famous for any great deeds. They are mentioned as a compliment to Augustus because his wife, Livia, was of that family.

Torquatus: killed his son for disobeying orders in war.

Camillus: after he had been exiled from Rome on false charges he was recalled to defeat the conquering Gauls, (around 390 B.C.) All these stories would be familiar to every educated Roman.

Monoecus: modern Monaco, one of Julius Caesar's strongholds. His daughter, Julia, was Pompey's third wife. After her death in 54 B.C. reconciliation between the two rivals was no longer possible. Most of Caesar's army came from Gaul, while Pompey recruited his from the eastern portion of the Mediterranean. Caesar claimed descent from Venus, through Aeneas, and thus was proclaimed a god after his death.

Corinth: destroyed by Mummius in 146 B.C.

Aeacus' son: here refers to Perseus, the last king of Macedon, who was defeated by Aemelius Paullus at the battle of Pydna in 168 B.C.

Cato: known as the censor for his stern conservatism. He was most famous for the words he always repeated before the Senate: "Carthage must be destroyed," and was thus in some ways responsible for the start of the third Punic War.

Cossus: an early Republican hero.

Gracchi: brothers, Tiberius was tribune and murdered in 133 B.C., Gaius in 121. Both tried to bring about reforms so that the common people would have a greater voice in government.

Scipios: a family famous for two hundred years of Republican history. The ones mentioned here are probably the two "Africani." Africanus the elder won the battle of Zama in 202 B.C. which ended the second Punic War. Africanus the younger destroyed Carthage in 146 B.C. at the end of the third Punic War.

Fabricius: rejected the bribes of Pyrrhus, 278 B.C., and later defeated him.

Serranus: nickname of Regulus, a general in the first Punic War. It comes from the latin word meaning to plant seed. The messengers who brought him the news that he had been elected consul found him planting in the fields.

Maximus: His whole name was Quintus Fabius Maximus Cunctator (the last name means the Delayer). Since the Carthaginian general Hannibal seemed impossible to beat, Fabius refused to meet him in a pitched battle. Instead he harried him in the rear and finally wore him out.

Marcellus: consul 222 B.C. killed the chief of the Insubrian Gauls. He is mentioned for the purpose of adding glory to his namesake, Marcellus. The second Marcellus was the son of Augustus' sister Octavia. He married in 25 B.C. the emperor's daughter, Julia, and was adopted by Augustus as his heir.

Caieta: town in Latium which got its name from being the burial place of Aeneas' old nurse, Caieta.

SUMMARY

Book VI may seem to imitate Homer's tale of Ulysses journey to the underworld (*Odyssey*, XI, 2-332), but actually it has a far grander scope.

1. Although there are many passages which are distinct echoes of Ulysses' experiences, (such as when he tries to embrace the spirit of his mother, but she, like a shadow or dream, flits out of his grasp) the weird, solemn, and philosophic mood is wholly Virgilian. Ulysses meets heroes and talks to them, but he is neither affected nor changed by what he sees. Aeneas, on the other hand, can not help feeling pity for the sufferings of the unhappy

souls he meets, and he changes from wavering and being insecure to possessing heroic spiritual strength.

2. The whole narrative is interwoven with symbolism. The **theme** of this symbolism is the relation of the world of myth to the world of history. Both worlds are controlled by Jupiter who represents order. Violators of world order suffer eternal punishment (such as the Titans who tried to overthrow Jupiter's rule). The **theme** of the interrelation of myth and history is not only a **theme** of Book VI, but also a central idea of the whole *Aeneid.* However, Virgil expresses it most clearly in the religious and philosophic atmosphere of this book. (It is possible that Virgil also thought of the journey through the underworld as symbolic of the tragedy of life.)

3. The third **theme** which transcends the simple narrative of the *Odyssey* is the glory of Rome, the **theme** with which the book closes. In the sense that the *Aeneid* is written to show the symbolic relation of history and myth to glorify Rome, Book VI contains the essence of the whole poem.

THE AENEID

BOOK VII

. . . .

(LINES 1-284.)

At the end of the last book Aeneas sets sail from Caieta. Book VII starts with the explanation for the harbor's name. Aeneas' nurse, Caieta, dies there, and the Trojans do not sail till they have completed the funeral rites for her. It is late afternoon when they finally get underway. Soon a full clear moon rises, casting its sparkling path of light upon the water. As the fleet sails northward it passes so close to the realm of the enchantress, Circe, that the Trojans can hear the howls of the men she has changed into lions, bears, wolves and other wild beasts. But Neptune is on guard and takes care to send favoring winds to speed them by the dangerous spot. As dawn comes up, Aeneas makes out the foaming mouth of the Tiber off to starboard, and gives the order to change course. They sail into the mouth of the peaceful river.

This land is ruled by king Latinus. Both he and his wife, Amata, are getting old, and have no son to inherit the kingdom. Their only child is a girl, Lavinia, whose hand is sought in marriage by all the neighboring princes. Of these the most renowned in valor and war-like deeds is Turnus, the young king of the Rutulians. The queen is anxious for Lavinia to marry this eligible suitor but, unfortunately, there are numerous oracles and omens which seem to be against the union. The most dreadful of these omens occurred when Lavinia and her father were sacrificing at the altar and the princess' hair caught on fire. When Latinus went to the oracle of his father, Faunus, to inquire the meaning, he was told that his daughter was destined to marry a foreigner, and that their descendants would bring eternal glory to his name. It wasn't long before Rumor had spread the story of the oracle throughout the surrounding countryside. By the time Aeneas lands everyone knows about it.

The travelers beach their ships and prepare something to eat. They make flat round cakes of cornmeal, on top of which they place the wild fruits they have gathered. It can hardly be called a banquet. In their hunger they eat the tasteless cakes too. All at once Iulus speaks up, almost without thinking: they are eating their tables. An awed hush falls over everyone as they remember the Harpy's prophecy. (Aeneas seems to have forgotten that it was the Harpy who made the prophecy, and says that he remembers his father, Anchises, saying the words.) In any case they consider it a good omen and Aeneas makes a special prayer to his father, and to the guardian spirit of the spot. The wine bowls are filled again and again.

The next day comes the task of building the city. One hundred chosen men go with Iulus as envoys to king Latinus. The rest remain with Aeneas to start work on the foundations. Iulus' embassy is impressed with the life and vigor of Latinus' city and eagerly seeks an audience with the king. When they see the carved images of Latinus' ancestors before the door to the temple they realize from what a long line and noble race he descends. The old king greets them graciously, and asks them whether a storm drove them to his shores, or whether they have strayed from their course. The spokesman for the Trojans, Ilioneus, steps forward and explains that they came to his land on purpose, as it was decreed by fate. He adds that they hope to settle, since they have been exiled so long from Troy, and to build their own city. Promising to be loyal allies, he offers Latinus relics which were saved from burning Troy: the golden bowl with which Priam poured libations at the altar, his scepter, and his crown. Latinus is deeply moved by the gifts, but even more by the thought that these Trojans may be the foreigners to whom the oracle referred; their leader may be his daughter's fated husband. So he gives them permission to settle, but asks especially that Aeneas come in person that he may welcome him. The embassy receives a parting present of three hundred horses with purple and gold trappings. For Aeneas there is a chariot with two beautifully matched horses. The future looks rosy indeed.

Comment

The most important aspect of this passage is the atmosphere of peace and friendship which pervades every line. All the events are favorable to the Trojans. Virgil has taken great pains to create this tranquil mood to heighten the contrast with the rest of the book.

NAMES AND PLACES

Circe: an enchantress who lured men to her island and then changed them into beasts. She was the daughter of the Sun and her horses were immortal. Ulysses in his adventures managed to outwit her (see *Odyssey,* X).

Erato: the muse of love poetry.

Tyrrhenian Band: another name for the Tuscans, a people living in Italy, who revolted against their tyrant Mezentius and joined Aeneas.

Faunus: father of Latinus, son of Picus, and grandson of Saturn. He was worshipped as the god of the fields and of oracles.

Albunea: a sulfurous spring.

Numicius: a small river in Latium flowing into the Tyrrhenian Sea.

Italus: an ancient god from whom the name Italy was thought to come.

Quirinus: another name for Romulus, the first king of Rome and the first religious diviner.

Aurunci: an early primitive tribe in Latium.

Corythus: an Italian hero, son of Jupiter, father of Iasius and Dardanus.

(LINES 285-571.)

Just when things seem to be going smoothly for everyone, Juno comes along. The sight of Aeneas and his friends rejoicing and building their city fills her with rage. In spite of all her efforts, storms at sea or marriage to Dido, the Trojans have managed to make it to Italy. Other gods have been able to take vengeance on those they hated, but she, the wife of the ruler of the universe is foiled at every turn. If the Olympian gods will not give her way, the she will try the powers of the underworld. Although she is well aware that she cannot change the decree of Fate (that Aeneas will wed Lavinia), at least she can put it off as long as possible. The goddess of war (Bellona) will be Lavinia's bridesmaid. To bring to pass these vindictive thoughts Juno summons the Fury, Allecto, from the underworld. She begs this hellish creature, dripping with snakes, to stir up strife and hate among Latinus' people: "Sow the wicked seeds of war."

How diabolically Allecto carries out the command! First she seeks out the queen mother, Amata, who wants Turnus for her son-in-law, in spite of her husband and the oracles. Standing over the queen with her hideous snakey tresses, Allecto takes one of the vipers hanging around her neck and thrusts it under a fold of Amata's robe. The queen is unaware of what is happening, but she grows more and more frenzied as the poison from the snake runs through her veins. At last the thought of her frustrated plans drives her wild, and she roams ranting and raving from one end of the city to the other calling on the other mothers to hear her wrongs. Only Bacchus is worthy to be her daughter's husband. Allecto drives her on, like boys driving a spinning top with their sticks, and all the Latin women are roused.

Having done as much harm as she could in that direction Allecto hastens to Turnus' palace. The young king of the Rutulians is peacefully sleeping. . . but not for long. The fiendish Allecto transforms herself into an aged priestess of Juno and appears to him in a dream. She tries to arouse his jealousy by taunting him that he is letting a foreigner walk off with his bride without a fight. All he has to do is to burn the Trojan's ships, kill their leaders, and Lavinia will be his. Turnus answers that he is well aware of what is going on but that it is not her business. She is supposed to attend to her sacrifices. Allecto, stung by these words, blazes with fiery anger. In the dream she changes back to her horrid form and the hissing of her innumerable snakes fills Turnus with terror. She hurls a torch at him and, sweating with agony, he starts from his sleep crying for arms. His whole spirit seethes with passion for war, the way a huge kettle boils fiercely when more and more wood is piled on the fire. He calls all the Rutulians to the defense of Italy.

Now Allecto turns to the Trojans. Her prey is young Iulus who has gone hunting, but her attack is directed at the hunting dogs. She fills them with madness for the scent of a stag which turns out to be no ordinary stag but the pet of the royal herdsman's daughter. Iulus takes true aim and hits the animal, but it manages to limp home. The daughter, wringing her hands in distress, calls upon her neighbors to help her find the villain who did such a wretched deed. The result is a pitched battle and the drawn swords glint in the sun as do the white crests of the waves, ruffled by an ever increasing wind. Blood flows on both sides and even the man who tries to make peace is killed. So Allecto returns to Juno in haughty triumph and points with pride to what she has achieved. If Juno will say the word she will spread the war even further. The queen of the gods, however, is a little fearful of the horrible Fury and tells her she has done enough. Anything more that needs to be done, she, Juno, can see to. Flying away on her hissing wings Allecto returns to the underworld.

Comment

This is one of the most artistically conceived passages in the *Aeneid.* The anger of Juno is mild beside the frenzy of Allecto. The pitch of the Fury's frenzy grows more intense with each visitation. The increasing insanity of Amata gives way before the terrible violence of Turnus' dream. This violence is in turn surpassed by the ferocious eagerness of battle. And dominating each scene is Allecto, a symbol of the demonic force of the historical world. What a contrast to the tranquility with which the book opened!

NAMES AND PLACES

Inachus: river near Argos, named for the first king and most ancient hero of Argos.

Pachynum: south-east promontory of Sicily. The gods were supposed to visit their favorite spots once a year, and in this passage Juno is going from Argos to Carthage.

Sigeum: the northwestern promontory in Asia Minor at the entrance of the Hellespont.

Calydon: a town in Aetolia in Greece famed for the wild boar which inhabited the nearby mountains. The goddess Diana sent the boar to ravage the town because its king, Oeneus, had failed to sacrifice to her. (*Iliad,* IX, 533 ff.)

Mars: not the starter of the battle between Lapiths and Centaurs, but thought of as the destroyer because he was the god of war.

Cisseus: a Thracian king, father of Hecuba, who dreamed before her son Paris was born that she would give birth to a burning torch. Juno says that Venus also has produced a torch because her son Aeneas will bring ruin on the new Troy by marrying Lavinia, as Paris did on old Troy by marrying Helen.

Phrygian Shepherd: Paris.

Acrisius: a king of Argos whose daughter, Danae, went to Italy, and married Pilumnus, an ancestor of Turnus. Ardea was the name of their city.

Trivia's Lake: modern Lago di Nemi where there was a grove of Diana.

Nar: a river famed for its sulfurous waters which flowed into the Tiber.

Velinus: a lake some seventy miles north-east from the Trojan camp.

Ampsanctus: a lake east of Naples which gave forth poisonous odors. It was therefore thought of as one of the entrances to the underworld.

(LINES 572-817.)

Once the battle has begun, there is no stopping it. As the wounded and the dead are brought home their wives and mothers cry for vengeance. Only Latinus resists the mass hysteria, and when he sees that his will has no effect among the people he resigns his rule. Hiding away he refuses to open the gates of the temple of

Janus because that would be an official declaration of war. So the goddess who caused the war, Juno, comes down from Olympus to perform this act. With w at eagerness do the people prepare for war! New forges are opened up so that more arms can be made. Even the horses seem proud to be going to war. All Italy blossoms with armed men.

The list of warriors is long and awesome. First there is the Tuscan, Mezentius, the scorner of the gods, with his handsome son, Lausus. Next comes Aventinus, son of Hercules and Rhea, striding along on foot, and swinging a terrifying lion skin. After him are the twins, Catillus and Coras, grandsons of a king of Argos, Amphiaraus. Then follows the king and founder of Praeneste, Caeculus, with his strangely armed battalion of slingers wearing helmets of wolf-skin. Next Messapus parades by accompanied by mail-clad warriors lustily singing marching songs. Then there is Clausus the Sabine with a host of Latin allies, and Halaesus, another man born in Argos and therefore eternal enemy of the Trojans. The tenth leader is aged Oebalus whose men use poisonous darts for weapons. A half barbarous tribe from the mountains led by Ufens comes next, and after them the priest, Umbro. He is sent by Archippus, king of the Marsi. Then Virbius, the son of exiled Hippolytus, (see below under names and places for his story) drives his horses and chariot over the plain.

At last Turnus appears, taller by a head than any of the other leaders. On his helmet is that most dreadful of fire-breathing beasts, a chimaera (lion-goat-dragon combination). His shield is emblazoned with a picture of Io being changed into a heifer. (She was the daughter of Inachus, the first king of Argos. Jupiter loved her, but she was changed into a heifer because of Juno's jealousy.) Rank on rank of armed infantry follow him.

Last of all the warrior maiden Camilla leads her troop of horse. As she goes by, the wives and mothers stare at her in amazement. Forward they all go to war; Turnus and his allies are prepared.

Comment

Virgil gives this catalogue of warriors for two reasons: one is in deference to Homer's catalogue of ships (*Iliad,* II, 484 ff.) The other is to give a feeling of buildup toward a frightful war. Juno, as always, stands as the symbol of the unleashed passion involved in fighting. It is important to notice that most of the Italian allies are only half civilized, in contrast to the followers of Aeneas.

NAMES AND PLACES

Getae: a tribe living near the mouth of the Danube conquered about 25 B.C. Virgil is praising the exploits of Augustus. Arabs in the next sentence refers to an expedition in 24 B.C.

Hyrcania: a province north-east of Persia inhabited by Parthians. The standards which the Parthians had conquered from Crassus in 53 B.C. were restored to the Romans in 20 B.C.

Gabine Cincture: a ceremonial manner of binding the toga so that it became shorter and closer around the body.

Helicon: a range of mountains near the Corinthian Gulf in Boeotia, sacred to Apollo and the Muses. Virgil invokes the muse before his catalogue of warriors as Homer does before the catalogue of ships.

Geryon: a three-headed monster, living on the island Erythea, near Gades, Spain. Hercules managed to steal his beautiful oxen. Tirynthian is an epithet of Hercules because he was brought up in Tiryns.

Sabelli: lesser tribe of the Sabines.

Tibur: a town not far from Rome, said to have gotten its name from Tiburtus, one of the three grandsons of Amphiaraus. It's modern name is Tivoli.

Homole And Othrys: mountains in Thessaly.

Gabii: an early Latin town not far from Rome. The legend of Caeculus' birth was that his mother was sitting by the fire and a spark jumped out and thus she conceived by Vulcan, but abandoned the child near the temple of Jupiter after it had been born.

Anagnia: the largest town of the Hernici about thirty-six miles east of Rome.

Amasenus: the god of the river of the same name located in Latium.

Fescennium, Capena, Mt. Soracte: all located in Etruria, north of Rome. Mt. Ciminus is west of Soracte. The Falisci inhabited a town near Fescennium.

Asian Pond: refers to the valley of the mouth of the Cayster river in Asia Minor, a favorite haunt of swans.

Quirites: inhabitants of Cures, a Sabine town; also the 'Men of Quirinus'.

Amiternum: another Sabine town. The next group of names all refer to either towns or rivers or mountains in the Sabine territory.

Hermus: a river in Asia Minor, flowing through Phrygia and Lydia.

Lycia: a southern district in Asia Minor.

Massicus: a mountain in Campania near the frontiers of Latium, famous for its wine.

Sidicini: a Campanian tribe.

Cales: a Campanian town.

Saticula: town north of Capua.

Sebethis: a nymph who lived in a small stream near Naples. Oebalus was not satisfied with his small kingdom of Caprea (Capri) and extended it to the north. The Teleboae were a pirate tribe who settled in Caprea.

Angitia: a goddess worshipped by the Marsi.

Fucinus: a lake in central Italy about fifty miles east of Rome.

Hippolytus: son of Theseus. His step-mother Phaedra fell in love with him, but he rejected her. In anger she accused him falsely to Theseus who had his son dragged to death by horses. Later, when he discovered Hippolytus' innocence, Diana persuaded the god of healing, Aesclepius, to restore his body. His name was changed to Virbius, and he was placed under the protection of the nymph Egeria, in the grove of Aricia.

Sicani: a tribe Virgil identifies with the Siculi who first inhabited Latium and then spread south into Sicily.

Sacrani: a mythical people.

Labicum: an ancient town in Latium.

Anxur: early name for Tarracina, a town southeast of Rome.

Feronia: an old Italian deity worshipped in Etruria and the Sabine region, goddess of fields and fertility, and freedom from slavery.

Satura: a marshy lake in Latium, formed by the Ufens and the Amasenus rivers.

Volsci: one of the tribes in Latium living to the south-east of Rome.

SUMMARY

Book VII begins what is commonly termed the "*Iliad* half" of the *Aeneid*. The first six books are considered the "*Odyssey* half." Virgil thought of it as parallel to Book I, but its development is directly reverse: Book I proceeds out of the violent storm at sea to the peace of Dido's court. Book VII goes from the tranquil Tibur setting at sunrise to the tumult of war. Allecto symbolizes the cruel power of the historical world as the storm is the cruel force of the natural world. The contrast between peace at the beginning and war at the end of the book is emphasized because of Virgil's own hatred of war, especially civil war. The whole book is permeated with the spirit of Allecto, the terrible personification of the unleashed passion of battle.

THE AENEID

. . . .

(LINES 1-369.)

Turnus has raised aloft the signal to arm, and from all over Italy men flock to his standard. Aeneas is only too well aware of this. Full of uncertainties about fighting against such great odds, he walks back and forth along the edge of the Tiber. As night falls he lies down to rest, and cut of the fog of the river a figure seems to rise and take the shape of the god of the river itself, Tiberinus. The kindly gray-haired old man speaks encouragingly to him, telling him not to dread the coming war. He promises him a good omen when he wakes up: Aeneas will see a white pig with a litter of thirty young around her, and they too will be white. This will be a sign that in thirty years Aeneas' son, Ascanius (also called Iulus), will build the city, Alba Longa. All that is necessary now is to find some allies. Further up the river is the city of Pallantium, named after king Evander's grandfather, Pallas. Evander is constantly at war with the Latin people and is sure to welcome

Aeneas as an ally. With a parting warning to sacrifice to Juno so that her anger may be appeased, the river god disappears into the mists from which he rose.

Getting up from the damp ground Aeneas looks around and sees that dawn is approaching. He is considerably heartened, however, by his vision and promises to remember the nymphs of the place and Tiberinus in his sacrifices from this day on. Then he hurries off to get two ships ready for the voyage upstream. As they are about to shove off, Aeneas notices a white pig and her brood on the bank. The promised omen! The hero catches the pig and performs a solemn sacrifice to Juno.

Then, greatly cheered, the Trojans bend willingly to the oars. For a day and a night and half the next day they row without resting, till they see in the distance the towers of Pallantium. As they make ready to beach their boats the young son of Evander, Pallas (who has come down to the river to participate in a festival in honor of Hercules), spies them, and demands to know who they are. Aeneas, holding out an olive branch as a sign that they have come in peace, tells him that they are Trojans, and hostile to the Latins. He asks Pallas to tell Evander that they have come to seek an alliance. Pallas is delighted with this information and the two go off arm in arm to find Evander.

Aeneas' first words remind Evander that they are distantly related, and that though the king's ancestors are Greek and his Trojan, they should be friends. Evander looks at Aeneas for a long time without speaking. Then his face brightens with a flash of recognition. How like his father Anchises he looks! Gladly he welcomes an alliance with the son of so noble a father. But before they can talk business, the festival of Hercules must be celebrated. Aeneas is invited to participate and the celebration starts off with a great feast. While they are eating, Evander tells him the reason for their veneration of Hercules. This famous hero had saved them from the terrible monster, Cacus, who had terrified their countryside with his plundering. When he stole some of Hercules' prize cattle he went too far and was finally caught and strangled. From that time on they have set aside one day a year in his honor. The festivities continue with dancing and singing tales of Hercules' great deeds. There is more food, and more wine and, after a final prayer, they return to the city. As they go, Evander fills Aeneas' ears with stories of the early days of the region and of the various kings who reigned. In the city itself he points out the important historical monuments. Finally they reach the Tarpeian hill (later called the Capitoline). There is a definite feeling of awe about its wooded summit, and all the peasants believe that some unknown god lives there. In reality, this early settlement, which Evander thinks of as a city, is little more than a primitive village. On the level ground at the foot of the hill, destined one day to be the great Roman forum, cattle are grazing. Evander's palace is only a hut. The bed he offers to his guest is made of leaves, its sheets are of bearskin. None the less, the great Hercules himself slept under the same roof, and Aeneas, though born to the luxury of a Trojan prince, does not scorn the humble home of this simple Italian king.

Comment

This passage symbolizes Aeneas' introduction to the customs and religious observances of Italy. It is only by leaving behind forever this Trojan ways that he can become a true ancestor of the Romans.

NAMES AND PLACES

Diomede: an old enemy of Troy who colonized Argyripa, or Arpi, in Italy.

Pallas: a king in Arcadia in Greece. His city was Pallantium, and his grandson Evander used the same name for the city he founded on the Tiber in Italy. Pallantium was later incorporated into Rome.

Amphitryon: supposed father of Hercules. He was the husband of Alcmene who bore Hercules by Jupiter in the guise of Amphitryon.

Atlas: one of the Titans who rebelled against Jupiter and was forced to bear the world on his shoulder. He is the common ancestor of Evander and Aeneas through his two daughters, Maia and Electra.

Daunus: king of Apulia and father of Turnus.

Geryon: a monster living in Spain. After Hercules slew him, he carried off his cattle and went to Italy. It was these same cattle that Cacus stole. The worship of Hercules was originally a family worship of the Potitia and Pinaria clans.

Salii: dancing priests, usually associated with religious festival to Mars. Here they take part in the worship of Hercules.

Troy And Oechalia: captured by Hercules, the first because Laomedon refused to give him his reward for killing a sea-monster; the second, a town in Thessaly, because its king, Eurytus, refused to give him his daughter Iole.

Eurystheus: king of Argos, for whom Hercules performed the twelve labors. Juno hated Hercules, as she did most of Jupiter's children who weren't her own also.

Hylaeus And Pholus: centaurs.

Cretan Monster: the bull which legend says he brought back alive to Eurystheus. All these are references to some of the twelve labors. He strangled the Nemean lion, carried back Cerberus, three-headed dog guarding the entrance to the underworld, and burned off the nine heads of the Lernian Hydra.

Typhoeus: frightful beast with a hundred heads, hands and eyes.

Carmentis: mother of Evander and a prophetess.

Asylum: built by Romulus to house refugees and thus increase the population of Rome. It was supposed to have been located between the two summits of the Capitoline hill.

Lupercal: a cave under the western side of the Palatine hill, connected with the worship of Lupercus, an Italian god of the country.

Lycaeus: a mountain in Arcadia where Pan, the Greek god of shepherds and flocks was born.

Carinae: name of a wealthy section of Rome.

(LINES 370-731.)

While Aeneas sleeps on his crude bed and all Italy is wrapped in darkness, Venus, his loving mother, begins to be concerned with the preparations for war. She decides to use her beautiful charms on Vulcan, the god of fire and forges, to persuade him to make the armor for her son. In the past he made arms for Achilles at his mother's, Thetis', request, and she, Venus, has not asked him for a single favor before this. She caresses him enticingly, kisses him, and his resistance vanishes. He promises to forge the strongest shield imaginable. Bright and early the next morning he departs for Sicily where the mighty forges of the Cyclops glow. There the smiths were working on a thunderbolt for Jupiter, and making a chariot for Mars. Vulcan tells them to stop everything and get to work on Aeneas' armor. At the same time that work on the shield begins, Evander and Aeneas get to work arranging the alliance. The king has the brilliant idea of enlisting the aid of the cities of Etruria which have revolted against the cruelties of their king, Mezentius. Hated for his murders and tortures (such as tying living bodies to a dead one, and letting them die in misery), he was finally driven out to seek refuge with his friend Turnus. Evander assures his guest that the Etruscans will willingly join him, not only because of wanting to kill Mezentius, but because an oracle has told them that a foreigner will come to lead them. In addition to the Etruscan army, Aeneas can have a token force led by Pallas, Evander's son, for to the old king, there is no one better suited for showing his son the arts of war. The treaty is on the verge of being settled when, in the cloudless sky, there is a tremendous clap of thunder. The hero looks up and thinks he sees arms flashing red in the blue air. Joyfully he tells his host that the thunder is a sure sign from his mother, Venus, that she is bringing the armor which she promised. Hastily Aeneas sacrifices to the guardian Lar of Evander's home, and then runs off to tell the rest of his men what has happened. A group of the best fighters he picks out to stay with him; the rest he sends back to his son, Ascanius, so that he may make proper preparations.

At this point, rumor of the approach of an advance Etruscan delegation reaches Pallantium. Aeneas decides to go and treat with them. As part of the embassy, Evander sends his son, Pallas, with a moving prayer to Jupiter for his safe return. Whatever happens, he wishes to die before he should hear news of his only son's death. With a mighty fanfare they set off for the Etruscan camp, and Pallas in the middle is seen to shine with the beauty of the Morning star.

As the delegation enters a wooded region, close to where the Etruscans are camped, Venus approaches, holding out the arms Vulcan has made. Mother and son embrace fondly, and then Aeneas turns to have a look at his exquisite armor. Never has he seen anything like it in his life. He fingers the thick plumes of the helmet with admiration, picks up the sword, trying it out for weight and balance. How well the ruddy colored bronze corselet fits him. How like the sun it shines! Even the greaves for his legs are crusted with gold. But more beautiful than all these is the fabulous shield. With infinite pains Vulcan had hammered into its surface scenes of Rome's future. Slowly, slowly, Aeneas turns the beautiful work of art around in his hands. His eyes pass over the picture of the wolf, which was to be the foster mother of the twins, Romulus and Remus. Next in order is the story of the Sabine women, carried off to be Roman wives. Then there is a picture of the king of the Sabines, Tatius, and Romulus, making peace. Here Horatius at the bridge is trying to prevent the Etruscans under Lars Porsenna from taking over Rome again. Then there is Manlius keeping the Gauls from the Capitoline after the hissing of the sacred geese had awakened him. There are scenes with Rome's enemies suffering in the underworld. In the very center is portrayed the glorious battle of Actium where the noble Roman, Augustus, conquers the oriental playboy, Antony. In the scene Augustus and his commander-in-chief, Agrippa, lead the fleet. Just beyond, the ships of Antony and Cleopatra can be seen, fleeing from the battle. All the gods of war are present, Mars, Bellona, and Discord. Venus takes up arms against Minerva; the Egyptian god, Anubis (worshipped in the form of a dog) attacks Roman Neptune. Pale Cleopatra and the weeping Nile-god are there, and finally Augustus Caesar himself, parading in triumph through the streets of Rome. Then he is seen consecrating all the temples, for his empire now extends to the farthest corners of their world. Proudly Aeneas raises high for all to see and admire the magnificent shield of Rome's future glory.

Comment

The description of the shield, the high point to which the book has been leading, comes directly from Homer's description of Achilles' shield (*Iliad,* XVIII, 478ff.) But there the similarity ends. With Virgil every scene is prophetic of Rome's history, while Homer describes the varied occupations of daily living. This points up the differences between the two poets. One writes to glorify a nation, the other, to glorify man.

NAMES AND PLACES

Nereus: father of the sea-nymph, Thetis, mother of Achilles.

Tithonus: husband of Aurora who asked Vulcan to make armor for her son Memnon.

Lipara: largest of a group of islands northeast of Sicily.

Lemnos: one of the larger islands in the Aegean, sacred to Vulcan because it was there that he landed when Jupiter hurled him from Olympus.

Tegea: important city of Arcadia, in Greece.

Maeonia: another name for Lydia where legend says the Etruscans originated.

Caere: also called by the older name Agylla, an Etruscan town.

Romulus and Remus: after floating down the Tiber in a make-shift cradle (they were abandoned by their mother who was a Vestal virgin) were found by a she-wolf who took them to her cave and nursed them till a shepherd boy rescued them.

Mettus: leader of the Roman allies from Alba Longa. In a battle when he was supposed to help the Romans, he refused to join, and later as punishment for treachery he was torn apart by chariots driven in opposite directions.

Tullus: third king of Rome who ordered Mettus' execution.

Cocles: refers to Horatius Cocles whose superhuman valor kept the whole Etruscan army under Lars Porsenna at bay on the other side of the bridge to Rome. Behind him the Romans destroyed the bridge. In the nick of time he jumped into the river and swam back to the Roman side and to safety.

Cloelia: A Roman virgin sent as a hostage to Porsenna. She escaped and swam back across the Tiber, but the Romans sent her to Porsenna again. He was so impressed that he set her free, along with several other hostages.

Cataline: conspired to overthrow the senate in 63 B.C.

Actium: one of the most famous battles in Roman history, between Augustus, and Antony and Cleopatra, actually more of a eaval battle than a land operation, fought off the Ambracian gulf on the northwest coast of Greece, September 2, 31 B.C. There was no town on the shore, only a temple to Apollo.

Sabaeans: a tribe living in Arabia.

Iapyx: the west-northwest wind blowing off the south of Italy and thus favorable to those crossing to Greece.

Triumph: in August 29 B.C. Augustus celebrated a triple triumph for victories in Dalmatia, Actium and Alexandria.

Mulciber: another name for Vulcan.

Leleges And Carians: peoples in Asia Minor.

Geloni: a Scythian people living near the Black Sea and south Russia.

Morini: a people dwelling on the coast of Gaul (France) opposite Britain.

Dahae: lived on the southeastern borders of the Caspian Sea.

Araxes: a river rising in Armenia and flowing into the Caspian. The force of its current was proverbial.

SUMMARY

The end of this book marks the end of the middle third of the poem. It closes with Aeneas lifting high the shield on which Roman history reaches its **climax** in the victory and triumph of Augustus. This symbolizes the fact that the hero has at last become mature enough to bear the destiny of Rome.

THE AENEID

BOOK IX

. . . .

(LINES 1-167.)

War at last! While Aeneas is away his enemies attack, for Iris, Juno's messenger takes care to inform Turnus of the Trojan leader's absence. As she vanishes into the rosy mist he raises his hands to her in prayer. Then comes the call to arms. The river of warriors is compared to the Nile or the Ganges in its mighty tide. Far in the distance the Trojans see the black cloud of dust rising toward the sky. With frantic speed they hurry behind the solid shelter of the wall of their settlement. It would be far more glorious to stay and fight before the walls, but the parting words of Aeneas before he left on his mission of alliance were not at any cost to attempt a pitched engagement. On his return he would tackle single handedly the enemy's champion. So Turnus, the passionate fighter, comes galloping up on his beautiful white stallion with an advance guard of twenty men, taunting the Trojans for their cowardice. Dramatically he hurls a javelin straight up into the sky, and then prances back and forth in front of the Trojan walls, His wild eagerness to get at the Trojans is likened to a starving wolf padding back and forth outside a sheepfold, not knowing how to get in. At last an idea strikes the impatient warrior. If he sets fire to the ships, surely the cowards will run out to save them. His followers, inflamed by Turnus' fury, with one accord throw flaming pine torches at the unprotected fleet. Clouds of black smoke billow skyward.

The mother of Jupiter, Cybele (also known as Rhea) sees the smoke in alarm. It was from her favorite mountain side that the pine timbers the Trojans used for their ships came. Surely Jupiter can do something to save her precious trees! Jupiter scolds her gently for trying to change fate, and then promises to change the ships into sea-nymphs. The fire has burned the ships cables, and as they drift out into the river, the pointed beaks of the bows seem to dive under the ripples and emerge in the form of beautiful nymphs. The Rutulians are terrified by this awesome sight and the horses whinny in fright. Only Turnus is calm; and he interprets the omen to their advantage: it is the Trojans who should be afraid, for now they cannot possibly flee. The Rutulian allies far outnumber the hated foreigners, and not even Venus herself will be able to help them. He, Turnus, does not need any trick, such as the horse the Greeks made at Troy, to get inside this puny settlement. Nor will he attack at night, but in full day light. But since most of this day is gone, the Rutulians retire to their camp and leave Messapus to set up a blockade of the walls. Soon the twilight is pierced by a ring of light from a hundred circling camp fires. The first day of battle is over.

Comment

This passage serves to show us the character of Turnus. He is a hero no less than Aeneas, yet somehow doomed to tragedy.

He represents passion in contrast to Aeneas' self-control in the last half of the *Aeneid,* as Dido did in the first half. But he still possesses the most essential qualities of a hero: beauty, noble birth, youth and courage. Before going into battle he faithfully performs the rites due the gods. All this heightens the tragedy of his passionate fury, which is continually illustrated by comparisons with wild animals. And always he is the source of the destructive element with his army.

NAMES AND PLACES

Thaumas: son of Earth and Sea, and father of Iris.

Doto And Galatea: sea-nymphs.

(LINES 168-502.)

Behind the walls the Trojans stand guard, but their courage is at low ebb. Aeneas is far away, and how can a messenger get through the enemy's blockade? Yet in the dark night, unknown to the rest of their companions, two close friends are forming a plan. Nisus, who guards one of the gates whispers excitedly to Euryalus of his burning longing to perform a deed of valor. Maybe this longing is sent by a god, or maybe each man makes such a longing into a god. Whatever the reason, he cannot stand remaining idle behind the walls when it is so essential to get word to Aeneas. Euryalus is fired by the idea and insists on going along. At first Nisus is against it because of Euryalus' youth, but finally the younger friend wins him over, and they set off to lay their plan before Ascanius and the other Trojan leaders. Ascanius is deeply impressed by their daring as is Aletes, the wise old war counselor. In fact the latter can not keep back the tears as he places his trembling hands on their shoulders. Aletes begs the two to name whatever reward they would like, but Ascanius interrupts to promise them greater treasures than they can dream of: two silver goblets worked with gold, two tripods, two talents of gold (a fortune for those days, close to $ 15,000) a bowl that had belonged to Dido herself, and if Turnus should fall in battle, his own beautiful white horse would be added to the prize. Euryalus has but one request. He has decided to depart on this perilous undertaking without telling his old mother, for she could not bear it. If fate should decree that he not return, let Ascanius comfort his bereaved mother. Such filial devotion brings the noble son of Aeneas to the verge of tears, and he promises that Euryalus' share of the reward will go to his mother, should something so dreadful happen. Then he fastens his own sword on the youth, while Nisus receives a protective lion skin from Mnestheus, and a helmet from Aletes. Accompanied by anxious prayers for their safety and the success of their mission, the two set off.

Everything goes according to plan, at first, that is. The night is moonless and they creep from shadow to shadow till they are in the very middle of the slumbering enemy. All around them are bodies stretched out on the ground, overcome with too much wine, or the weary excitement of the day, or both. No one is awake to see them. Burning with revenge, they go from body to body, piercing one through the belly, cutting off the head of another, more like a lion mangling his victims in a sheepfold, than two civilized human beings. Indeed, Euryalus becomes completely swept away by lust for more blood. But Nisus catches hold of himself, recollecting the sacred nature of their mission. Already the shadows are less dark, and the sky is graying with the coming dawn. They must go now, while there is still a chance of making it to Aeneas. The younger man can barely manage to tear himself away from such a triumph. With almost childlike eagerness, he puts on as much of the armor of the men he has slain as he can: the sword-belt on one, and the helmet with lovely waving plumes of another. Sadly he leaves behind all sorts of arms, gold and silver bowls, beautiful carpets, and other priceless treasures. But the shining helmet was to be his undoing, for as they head for the path by the river leading to Pallantium, a troop of three hundred horsemen bear down upon them as they seek to hide in the brush along the road. They are coming to Turnus with messages and help from king Latinus. Three-hundred against two are pretty frightful odds. Still if they can reach a little footpath off to the left, they may have a faint chance of avoiding being seen. But the leader of the horsemen, Vulcens, catches sight of something, the plume of the helmet, white in the uncertain shadows and cries out for them to halt.

Fear gets the better of wisdom and the friends flee in opposite directions. Euryalus, being younger and terribly inexperienced, quickly looses his way, doubles back on his tracks without knowing it, and is captured. Nisus has better luck in eluding his pursuers, and could have gotten away all together if his tremendous love for Euryalus had not made him turn around. Realizing that Euryalus is nowhere in sight, he retraces his steps toward the sound of the scuffle. He too is now lost, for what possibly can one man do against so many? It no longer matters. All that does matter is that Euryalus shall not die unavenged. Forming a prayer to Diana under his breath, he dodges from bush to bush ever closer, till he comes upon Vulcens, just as he is driving home his sword into Euryalus body. Two others has Nisus already slain in his search for Vulcens. Now it is Vulcens' turn! As Euryalus rolls over, lifeless Nisus plunges his sword right through the skull of his friend's slayer. Seconds later he too is killed. The two, inseparable in life, are now together forever. But victory has its price. The mourning embassy from Latinus, carrying the body of their dead leader, enters the Rutulian camp, which is also filled with grief for the countless men slain by the hands of the two Trojans. Nor does news of such a slaughter remain unknown for long. For Turnus, with the cruelty inspired by war, lifts high on sharp pikes the two heads of the reckless Trojans. The grief-stricken mother of Euryalus is almost the first to hear the grim story. Inconsolably she attacks heaven with her cries of anguish. Her son is not only slain by the enemy, but she cannot even have the headless corpse to bury with the honor due a hero. Just as she is about to jump off the wall into the thick of the enemy, two Trojans at Ascanius' command carry her back to her room unconscious.

Comment

The Nisus and Euryalus story is one of the most vivid in the whole *Aeneid,* and also one of the most romantic, in the sense that friendship is idealized and exalted, at the expense of wisdom and prudence.

NAMES AND PLACES

Hyrtacus: married Priam's first wife, Arisba, when Priam married Hecuba.

Assaracus: a Trojan ancestor; his Lar would thus be considered the guardian deity of the whole Trojan race.

Arisba: a town in Asia Minor which sent allies to Troy.

Creusa: Ascanius' mother, Aeneas' first wife who died at Troy. (See *Aeneid,* II.)

(LINES 503-818.)

Now the piercing notes of battle trumpet rend the air as with ever increasing force the Rutulians redouble the attack. Scaling ladders are set against the walls, only to be pushed back by the Trojans. All along the top of the wall the Trojans roll down great stones. But especially fierce is the fighting in front of the high tower on the wall of the settlement, as the defenders there have tremendous superiority in being so high. Their arrows have deadly effect among the Rutulians. Suddenly Turnus grabs a blazing torch and hurls it with almost superhuman strength at the wooden structure. Fanned by the wind it soon is nothing but a mass of flames. Then it comes crashing to the ground. Two of the Trojans are thrown into the ranks of the enemy: Helenor is killed instantly, but Lycus, attempting to scale the wall and reach the outstretched hands of his comrades, is torn down by triumphant Turnus. Again and again the Italian allies come on, under their heavy round shields, one man right beside the next, the whole formation looking like a giant tortoise.

In front of another part of the wall parades an insolent upstart, Numanus. Giving himself airs because he has just married Turnus' younger sister, he shouts all kinds of jibes at Ascanius: he mocks him because of his style of clothes hinting that he cannot be a man if he wears a helmet with ribbons on it, and purple embroidered gowns; he and all the Trojans must be women since they do not even dare come out and fight. The Italians breed a race of men, toughening them in infancy by washing them in the ice-cold river, teaching them to hunt, and to master every tool and weapon made of iron. Trojans are only good for dancing; fighting is not for women! Ascanius can stand it no longer, and vowing a steer to Jupiter once a year till he dies, if the king of the gods will guide his arrow, he takes aim, and shoots the proud boaster through the head. Cheers go up from the ranks of the Trojans! But Apollo thinks that Ascanius is too young to be fighting the battles of men, and leaving Olympus, disguised as the boy's old tutor, Butes, remarks to him that his shot was fabulous, but there will be plenty of opportunity for him to fight when he is older. The Trojans who are standing around sense that a god spoke the words, and restrain Ascanius in his eagerness. But the youth's feat fires the weary Trojans as they return to the fray.

At that moment, however, two foolhardy young men take it upon themselves to open the gates and charge the Rutulians. This was the one thing they had been strictly commanded not to do, and its results were nearly fatal to the Trojans. For far from being able to rush out, they are immediately charged by the outnumbering Rutulians. Turnus himself, fighting tirelessly in one part of the battle, hastens to the breach. The Trojans fall back in terror before the fire in his eyes and his death-dealing sword. The sound of falling bodies is worse than the crash of a landslide sending boulders rumbling into the sea. None can stand against the might of Turnus. The brilliance of his armor reflecting the sunlight is almost blinding. The blood-red plumes of his helmet make him seem twice as tall as he is. Finally Pandarus, a tall man in his own right, ventures to take him on. With a calm smile on his face, Turnus raises his sword and cleaves Pandarus' skull in half. The valiant Trojan topples to the ground, the halves of his head dangling weirdly. The Trojans scatter in terror as Turnus advances. In fact, if he had not been carried away by mad lust for killing, he could have opened the gates of the settlement. The Trojans had closed them behind him when he had far outdistanced the rest of the Rutulians. But victory has gone to his head and he looks only for the next man to kill.

Finally the Trojan leaders in despair hold a war council, and Mnestheus, the leader, shouts out stinging words to his men: are they going to let one man, all alone against so many, go unscathed? Where is their courage, their love for the gods and for Aeneas? These words turn the tide, and step by step they press Turnus back toward the river like a lion hemmed in on all sides by hostile spears. Even so they suffer two setbacks until the whole Trojan army is massed against the one mighty warrior. Only when he is overwhelmed on all sides, when the rain of arrows and stones on his helmet and shield becomes deafening, and the blood-red plumes of his helmet are cut in two, does the thought of flight occur to him. With a headlong leap, he plunges into the Tiber, armor and all, and escapes back to his army.

Comment

The pace of battle in this passage moves almost faster than the poet. There is a horrible fascination in the bloody exploits of Turnus. Though he is the villain representing the demonic fury of battle and the cruelty of war, it is impossible not to admire him.

NAMES AND PLACES

Calliope: muse of **Epic** poetry.

Symaethus: located on the east coast of Sicily.

Palici: twin gods of Sicily, sons of Jupiter and the nymph, Thalia, who was Vulcan's daughter. They were worshipped in the neighborhood of Mt. Aetna.

Dindymus: a mountain in Phrygia, sacred to Cybele.

Sarpedon: prince from Lycia, ally of the Trojans, killed by Patroclus.

SUMMARY

This is the book of thundering war in which Turnus is the star. It is also the book of wild animal similes: the lion, the wolf, the eagle. We may wonder how Virgil, a poet of pathos and insight, with seemingly tender sensibilities, could write such bloody battle scenes. And some critics may argue that the scenes lack the vitality and primitive power of Homer. They are still full of tremendous **realism**, symbolic of the bloodstained pages of Rome's history. By showing the horrors of war, Virgil makes the strength and glory of the peace which Rome finally brought to the world, under Augustus, even greater.

THE AENEID

BOOK X

....

(LINES 1-117.)

Meanwhile on Olympus, Jupiter becomes very upset at the continued fighting and decides to call a council of the gods as he had commanded that the Trojans and Rutulians should be friends. Unfortunately, like so many councils, it accomplishes little more than giving the rival parties a chance to quarrel in public. Venus naturally blames the war on Turnus, broadly hinting that Jupiter's wife has had a great deal to do with it. Still, if her grandson Ascanius is spared, she will be satisfied. Juno retorts that it isn't her fault if Aeneas attempts to marry someone else's promised bride (Lavinia). Now was she to blame that the Trojan prince, Paris, carried off Sparta's princess, Helen. It wasn't her fault either that the Trojan war started in the first place. All the rest of the gods take sides, and the dispute goes from bad to worse. Finally in disgust, Jupiter throws up his hands, saying that he will take neither side. Whatever happens is in the hands of Fate.

Comment

These opening lines in many ways seem to be an unnecessary imitation of Homer's council of the gods (*Iliad,* beginning of IV and VIII). The only result is that Jupiter says he will not interfere. The power of fate is above the power of the gods.

NAMES AND PLACES

Alps: a reference to Hannibal's crossing in 218 B.C when he led the Carthaginian forces.

Arpi Or Argyripa: town in Apulia in Italy, founded by Diomede who settled there after the Trojan war. He was the son of Tydeus and wounded Venus when she rescued Aeneas from him (*Iliad* V, 336).

Amathus: town in Cyprus beloved by Venus.

Pilumnus: ancient Italian god.

Venilia: a sea-nymph, mother of Turnus; sister of Amata, the wife of Latinus.

(LINES 118-660.)

Back among mortals, the battle rages fiercely, and the sorely tried Trojans begin to loose hope. But unknown to them help is at hand, for Aeneas approaches. With him is the small force of Evander and the huge army of his Etruscan allies. All night long the ships have been speeding toward the beleaguered settlement. At the head of one division of the Etruscan army is Ocnus, whose native city, Mantua is the head of a league of twelve cities. (Virgil inserted this bit to glorify his own home town, which was Mantua.) Guided by the moonlight the men bend tirelessly to the oars. All at once the fleet is surrounded by beautiful sea-nymphs. They are the hero's old ships which Cybele had changed into sea-nymphs to save from being burned by Turnus. One of them, Cymodocea, wakes Aeneas from his brief rest to tell him what has happened to those he left behind and to warn him about Turnus. Then she and her nineteen sisters swim behind the boat so that they skim along twice as fast. Aeneas breathes a prayer of thanks to Cybele for this wonderful omen.

By daybreak they are in sight of the settlement. A shout of joy rises from the throats of the exhausted Trojans. Their beloved leader has returned. Strengthened by fresh hope, they fight back fiercely. But Turnus, with brilliant strategy, decides to abandon the attack on the walls and to defend the shore instead. If he prevents the reinforcements from landing, the Trojans are doomed. But he gets there too late to hinder the first of Aeneas' men. Some leap into the shallow water as it ebbs back from the beach, others take their turn scrambling down the gangplanks. On and on they come, Aeneas at their head. Against him, none can fight, and live. Aeneas uses up all his weapons so fast that he has to send his friend, Achates, back to the ships for more. And in another part of the battle his young ally, Pallas, is fighting just as nobly. Having met tremendously stiff opposition the force given by Evander starts to give way. But Pallas spurs them on with high words, and gallops into the thickest part of the fighting. Every enemy falls before him, and courage returns to his men. Nearer and nearer he gets to where his counterpart among the Rutulians, Lausus, is putting on an equally good show of bravery. Just as Pallas and Lausus are about to meet, however, Turnus comes riding up in his war chariot, claiming that he alone has the right to fight

Pallas. Alas for Pallas! For all his noble nature he is no match for peerless Turnus. The two size each other up and Turnus attacks like a lion a bull. Pallas throws his spear first, praying to Hercules to make it go true. But though it does pierce the armor at the shoulder, Hercules is powerless to go against the decree of Fate. For this day of battle is Pallas' appointed day of death. The power behind Turnus' huge oak spear is far greater. Its tip penetrates the armor through to the heart. But Turnus, in honor of his noble adversary, does not mangle the corpse but takes only the beautifully worked sword belt as his spoil. With loving care his friends bear the dead hero's body from the field.

News of Pallas' death drives Aeneas to his wildest deeds. Left and right he cuts the Rutulians down. He grasps one wretch who begs for mercy by the plume of his helmet and, bending his head way back, runs his sword through his neck. His weapons are warm with ever fresh blood. He attacks two brothers who come riding up in their chariot, drawn by two white horses. The first he pierces through the groin as he is about to take aim with his spear and the Rutulian falls over onto the ground. His terrified brother begs Aeneas to spare him, but the raging hero hacks him in two. Everywhere he looks for Turnus, but the latter is nowhere to be found because Juno, fearing that Aeneas might kill her dear Turnus, begged Jupiter for permission to get Turnus out of the fight. Jupiter grudgingly consented, and so Juno invented a ghost to look like Aeneas. And this she causes to flit around the scene of battle, so that Turnus, on seeing what he thinks is Aeneas, pursues it far from the fighting, down to a waiting ship, which is also part of Juno's scheme. As Turnus is about to run the phantom through, it disappears before his eyes. Filled with shame because he will now be thought a coward, Turnus bitterly reproaches Jupiter for pulling such an unfair trick. Nor can he get back to the battle, for Juno has cut the ship's cable and he is far out to sea. The thought of the army which has followed him so faithfully fills him with despair. No wonder Aeneas cannot find him.

Comment

In this book Aeneas is the star warrior, even as Turnus was in Book IX. But here we also get a fine picture of Turnus' character. He is not just a proud, cruel killer. His heroic qualities show forth at their best when he refuses to rob the dead Pallas of more than his sword belt, and when despair comes upon him at the loss of his honor. That he was tricked makes him tragedy all the greater. There is tragedy in the death of Pallas too, because his noble nature seems to attract such a destiny.

NAMES AND PLACES

Oricum: town in Illyria on the Greek coast. The district was famous for its turpentine, or terebinth, trees.

Ida: the figurehead of the ship is a replica of Mt. Ida with Cybele's lions at its base.

Chalybes: a people of Pontus who lived near the shore of the Black Sea and were famous for their iron work.

Cycnus: father of Cinyras and Cupavo, beloved of Phaethon. When the latter was destroyed by Jupiter, Cycnus' grief was so great that he was changed into a swan.

Strymon: the river forming the boundary between Thrace and Macedonia.

Sirius: the dog-star whose ascendency in the late summer was associated with diseases of that dry and unhealthy time.

Lichas: children who were saved alive from dead mothers were dedicated to Apollo as the god of healing (also the sun-god).

Sword-Belt: worn over the shoulder. Pallas' was engraved with the story of the murder of the sons of Aegyptus by the daughters of Danaus.

(LINES 661-908.)

But though Juno has dishonorably removed Turnus from the fight, Jupiter raises up another warrior from the ranks of the Rutulians, equally as fierce. This is Mezentius, the deposed king of Etruria, whose cruelty is well known through the land. Like a lion maddened with hunger which spies a stag, leaps upon it, and then crouches over the carcass, gloating, with gory fangs, so does Mezentius leap at the Trojans who come against him. And Aeneas, since Turnus has disappeared, seeing this terrible havoc in the Trojan ranks, goes after him. For this encounter, Mezentius is ready and eager. Proudly he tells his son, Lausus, who is fighting at his side, that he shall wear the armor of Aeneas as Mezentius' trophy of battle. He hurls a spear at Aeneas, but it glances off the hero's shield, and kills another. Aeneas in his turn hurls his, and Mezentius is hit in the groin. Lausus cries out in horror at the sight of blood gushing from his dear father. But the older man fights on, though painfully with slowly retreating steps. Then, before his father can stop him, young Lausus leaps between pursuer and pursued, protecting his father's withdrawal with his own shield. Nor are his blows light, but Aeneas fends them off till Lausus has spent all his energy.

Then, and only then does the Trojan leader press the attack. In an instant he buries his sword up to the hilt in the young man's body. At the sight of so young a man lying dead before him, an irrepressible groan escapes from the hero's lips, for the image of Ascanius fills his eyes. He cannot take the youth's armor, his right as prize of victory. In deep compassion he helps Lausus' friends lift up the lifeless body so they can carry it off the field, wailing as they go. The sound of their cries reaches Mezentius as he nurses his wound by the Tiber, his breath coming in short painful gasps. With bitter words he curses himself for letting the son fight the father's battle. The death of his only child touches the cruel tyrant as nothing else could. Wild with grief he crawls to his feet and manages to pull himself up onto his horse. As the horse paws nervously at the strangely unbalanced weight on his back, Mezentius talks encouragingly to the poor beast in low tones. Then, charging back to the densest fighting, he calls loudly for Aeneas: "I come, about to die, but first I carry these as gifts." Javelin after javelin he hurls at the wary Trojan as he circles round him, but his strength wanes, and the weapons bounce off the shield harmlessly. Finally Aeneas, tired of waiting and turning round and round, strikes the horse a mighty blow on the head. The beast rears up, pitching off his rider, and then rolls over on top of him. Unsheathing his sword Aeneas makes ready to finish the Etruscan. Waiting only to hear his foe's last request that he be properly buried, since his own people hate him, Aeneas plunges the sword through his throat.

Comment

This passage gives a wonderful portrait of Mezentius, the hated tyrant of Etruria. He is compared to a barren crag that resists all the buffets of the storms, to a wild boar which no one dares face, to a lion leaping on a stag, to a whirlwind, and to a giant.

135

In contrast to him is Aeneas, who seems to have lost the savage ways with which he fought in the first part of the book, for his treatment of Lausus shows his compassionate nature.

NAMES AND PLACES

Vesulus: one of the Italian Alps-Monte Viso, whence rose the Po river.

Corythus: an Italian hero, father of Dardanus; also a city in Italy.

Orion: a giant huntsman changed into a constellation by Diana.

SUMMARY

Perhaps the true hero of Book X is Fate, for neither Jupiter's calm detachment, nor Juno's passionate partisanship can change the outcome of the war. Pallas and Lausus, the noblest of the young men on each side must die, and Juno's spiriting Turnus away has only put off the day of his death, as well she knows. For a brief period Aeneas is almost a Homeric hero, caught up in the present by the madness of war. But when, at the death of Lausus, he thinks of his own son, his destiny and future come back to him, and he is filled with pity for the young life that is to know no future. Thus the book where Fate is the hero ends on a note of true pathos.

THE AENEID

. . . .

(LINES 1-444.)

Both sides have had enough of war. There are so many dead! Envoys from Turnus' camp come seeking a truce to bury their dead at the very moment when the Trojans are in the middle of the ceremony in honor of Pallas. Around the bier made of oak twigs (the oak was sacred to Jupiter) and arbutus shoots (or wild strawberry tree, famous for its shade) the Trojan women wail, their long hair unbound as a sign of mourning. Even in death he is still beautiful, like a violet that has been picked but has not yet wilted. Sorrowfully Aeneas covers the body with a priceless robe made by Dido herself of purple cloth worked with gold. Then the sad procession sets out for Pallanteum to return the corpse to Evander. Interrupted by the Rutulian envoys, the line of Trojan men and women comes to a halt while Aeneas talks courteously to the emissaries.

Gladly he grants the twelve days truce they seek, and would willingly end the war if he could: it was not of his seeking. One of the Rutulians, Drances, who has never been in favor of Turnus' war, promises to do all he can to smooth things out with Latinus and to bring about an alliance with Aeneas; let Turnus find an alliance somewhere else. With these words they depart, and the funeral procession continues on toward Pallanteum.

Long before it gets there, however, the news of his son's death reaches the ears of Evander. Rumor has flown on ahead, and as the Trojans get closer to the city they see a long line of Evander's citizens, carrying flickering torches, winding out to meet them. Stumbling at the head of the group is the old king himself, his face streaked with the tears bewailing the cruelty of fate. He falls prostrate on the bier moaning that life has no more meaning. All he wants are vengeance for Pallas and his own death.

All over the fields smoke from the countless funeral pyres rises toward the sky. Latins, Rutulians, Trojans, made allies by death as they cannot be in life, mourn their dead.

An additional cause for grief then comes to Turnus: Diomede has refused to join with them. Even though he fought against the Trojans long ago, he wants no part of fighting them now. Aeneas is far too noble. In fact, Diomede suggests that rather than giving himself gifts to cement an alliance, they should be presented to the Trojan leader. King Latinus is more than ready to follow this suggestion. His kingdom is large enough for Trojans and Latins alike. Happily would he give them a tract of land to settle in or, if they wish to go elsewhere, timber to build new ships. Drances speaks out in favor of Latinus' proposal, in keeping with his promise to Aeneas. One and all, the Latins long for peace and if the king's daughter, Lavinia, is given in marriage then the peace will be certain.

But the thought of such a disgraceful peace is more than Turnus can bear. He jumps up from his seat at the council and taunts Drances for his honeyed words; always the talker and never the doer! There have been rumors that he is a coward. Well, they will see who is the real man, the one afraid to fight, or the one who seeks glory in war. For the sake of Italy and his ancestors he is prepared to die, if necessary. One sure ally they do have, the warrior queen Camilla.

Comment

The moving description of the funeral for Pallas in this passage shows how deeply Aeneas (and thus Virgil) was affected by the bitterness of war. Aeneas' sensitivity to tragedy at the beginning of the passage is in sharp contrast to Turnus' love of glory, whatever the cost.

NAMES AND PLACES

Parthasia: district in Arcadia in Greece where Evander came from.

Trophy: a victor's trophy was usually the trunk of some tree decked with the armor of the man he killed.

Diomede: went with eighty ships to the Trojan war, and was the bravest of the Greeks, next to Achilles. After the war he left Argos and was driven by a storm to the east coast of Italy. There legend says that he founded many cities, among them Argyripa, or Arpi.

Iapygia: part of Apulia in southeast Italy.

Garganus: a promontory on the east coast of Italy, the modern Gargano.

Caphereus: a promontory in Euboea in Greece where the Greek ships were wrecked returning from Troy. Athena (Minerva) sent a storm and the king of Euboea, Nauplius, hung out false lights to guide the fleet onto the rocks.

Proteus: one tradition makes him king of Egypt, and thus Virgil means the eastern end of the Mediterranean. (See *Odyssey*, IV;81).

Neoptolemus: also called Pyrrhus, son of Achilles, killed at Delphi, and his kingdom in Epirus divided, part of it going to Helenus (see *Aeneid* III, 325 ff).

Idomeneus: king of Crete, and one of Helen's suitors (see *Aeneid* III, 122 ff).

Lord Of Mycene: Agamemnon, killed by his wife Clytemnestra, who was urged to the deed by her lover Aegisthus.

Calydon: ancestral home of Diomede in Aetolia in Greece.

(LINES 445-915.)

Into the middle of this council, where there only seemed to be disagreement, a messenger runs to say that the Trojans are advancing with their Etruscan allies. This is the chance Turnus has been looking for. Ironically he asks the assembled group if they are going to sit quietly talking peace while their city is being invaded. In a flash the council chamber is empty. Only Latinus is still angry with himself that he had not taken steps at the beginning to unite his daughter with Aeneas. No good could come from this renewed fighting. His queen, Amata, and Lavinia, along with the crowd of women, go to the temple of Minerva to pray for victory. Other women, and boys too, make for the walls of the city to aid in defense, so thinned are the ranks of the Latins and Rutulians.

Turnus, glad for action at last, charges out the gate like a powerful stallion bursting from the imprisonment of his stall, who heads for the open pasture, neighing in wanton joy. The warrior maiden, Camilla, gallops to meet him, and suggests that he stay by the walls to guard the city while she and her Volscian cavalry engage the light-armed horse of Aeneas and the Etruscans. Turnus decides to let her face the cavalry while he goes and ambushes the infantry as they come through a narrow pass. He is full of admiration for Camilla, as well he might be: she was hardened to war from infancy. When her father, Metabus, was driven by the enemy from his city he took with him in his flight his baby daughter. Unable to swim the flooded river encumbered by the child, he tied her to the middle of his spear-shaft and hurled it across, plunging in and swimming over just in time to save her. Safely beyond the reach of his pursuers, he took over the care of the tiny baby himself, and fed her wild mare's milk. Her first playthings were a bow and arrows, and while still a small child she mastered the art of the slingshot. In men she showed no interest but worshipped only Diana, the virgin goddess. No wonder she is such a magnificent fighter.

The whole plain now bristles with the spear points glinting in the bright sun. Spurring their horses on, the two armies charge toward each other and then, abruptly, rein in barely a spear's throw apart. The sky is blackened with the shower of spears and arrows. But the Latins fall back and flee toward the city. Suddenly they wheel about and attack their pursuers, who are routed in their turn. So goes the ebb and flow of battle. In the heart of the fighting rides Camilla, one breast bare, wielding her battle-ax, and shooting arrows even in retreat. She is more than the equal of any Amazon, or even that most famous of Amazonian queens, Hippolyta. Many a Trojan bites the dust because of her faultless aim.

Just then as the Etruscans seem to be losing heart, their leader, Tarchon, goads them into action by saying that they are cowards to be defeated by a woman. Like lightning, like an eagle, he goes through the ranks killing right and left. The sight of such magnificent fighting inspires the young Etruscan Arruns to go after Camilla. As Camilla recklessly pursues a Trojan priest, Arruns stalks her, praying all the while to Apollo. Suddenly she raises her arm to throw the spear, but Arruns hurls his first, catching her unguarded with uplifted arm. And while the Etruscan, flushed with victory, looses his head and runs from the scene, the warrior maiden vainly tries to pull the spear out, but the barb has gone too deep. Just before she topples lifeless from her horse she gasps out a last message to her sister to tell Turnus what has happened. He must return and defend Laurentum.

With Camilla dead, the Latin cause is lost. It is not a Rutulian who slays Arruns in revenge, or a Volscian fighting maiden, but one of the handmaids of the goddess Diana, Opis, performs the deed. Forgotten by his comrades he lies in the dust, pierced by an arrow of the virgin goddess. When the news of the disaster reaches Turnus he abandons his ambush and speeds toward the doomed city. Minutes later Aeneas and his troops come through the unguarded pass. Only the coming of the night prevents the two armies from engaging. But the die is cast, and the next rise of the sun will bring the final outcome.

Comment

In this passage Camilla seems to personify the bright aspect of war, even as Turnus is the cruel aspect. The description of Camilla and her cavalry is completely original with Virgil, and considered by many to be his best battle scene.

NAMES AND PLACES

Privernum: a city in Latium on the Amasenus river.

Thermodon: a river in Pontus, Asia Minor, in the homeland of the Amazons.

Penthesilea: another queen of the Amazons who fought on the side of the Trojans. She was killed by Achilles.

Gortynia: town in Macedonia.

Soracte: mountain in Etruria where there was a temple to Apollo.

The rites consisted of walking barefoot through hot embers.

SUMMARY

This book leaves the reader almost breathless. It starts with the slow sad dignity of the funeral procession, and ends with the mad, headlong flight of the remnant of the Rutulian army and the massacre at the gates as they crowd upon one another in their panic to escape the Trojans. Like a bright flash of light, Camilla appears in the last section, pointing up the way Virgil was torn between the tragic bitterness of war in real life, and the shining glamor of war in myth.

THE AENEID

BOOK XII

....

(LINES 1-613.)

Turnus now is the only hope. Only through him can Laurentum be saved. Still believing in his mission to preserve the nations of Italy as they existed before the Trojans' arrival, he burns with the desire for revenge, and madness increases. Picture a lion of the African jungle, who becomes truly ferocious only when wounded by the hunters. Turnus' wound is to his pride, but the pain is just as terrible. He entreats King Latinus, with mounting impatience, to set up the agreement that he and Aeneas may contend for their countries' honor, and for victory, in single combat. But Latinus is still for appeasement. Why should he not make an end of war while Turnus is alive, if he is willing to become an ally of the Trojans with Turnus dead? But his attempt at appeasement only increases the warmonger's passion. If he must die, at least death will bring him fame. His loving mother, however, intrudes in an emotional outburst: he must not fight in single combat with terrible Aeneas, for, if he dies, she will kill herself. Beautiful Lavinia, too, adds her tears to those of his mother. Turnus is appalled at the scene they are making. Tears are no fit accompaniment for a hero going into battle! Paying no heed to anyone, he summons his beautiful white horses, dons his armor, picks up the sword that Vulcan made for him, and seizes his spear, all with the grim frenzy with which a bull prepares to attack a tree trunk.

At the same time Aeneas makes equal preparations, rejoicing in his heart that the war is to be settled by single combat. The two sides troop together to confirm the agreement and make it binding. On one side Rutulians, on the other, Trojans, are marshaled with great pomp. Turnus brandishes two spears as he stands in his war chariot, drawn by the matched white horses. On the Trojan side, Aeneas strides forward, wearing his god-made armor which shines with blinding brilliance. Each combatant comes to the altar and makes the proper sacrifice. Aeneas speaks out a mighty prayer, calling on Sun, Earth, Jupiter, Juno, Mars, and Floods and Fountains as witnesses. If Turnus wins, the Trojans will retreat to Evander's city. His son, Ascanius (Iulus) will leave the land forever. They will never reopen the war. But if Aeneas wins, the victorious Trojans will be merciful, not seeking to rule the conquered, but living together as equals. And the city they build shall be named after his father-in-law's daughter, Lavinia.

The compact seems sacred enough, but Juno is always afraid for her dear Turnus. She still wants to save him if she can. Leaving Olympus, she seeks out the nymph of a fountain nearby. Her name is Juturna, and she is a sister of Turnus. Jupiter was her lover at one time, but because of her relationship to Turnus, she is the only one of Jupiter's amours whom Juno does not hate. Juno explains that she is prevented by Jupiter from doing anything more to help Turnus, but perhaps Juturna can think of something. She can, and does. Assuming the disguise of a noble Rutulian, Camers, she spreads dissatisfaction among Turnus' followers. Latinus is in the middle of making his vow to the gods. He invokes Earth, Sea, Stars, Apollo and Diana, and the gods of the underworld. Then he places his hands upon the altar, and the two leaders sacrifice the sacred animals to make the treaty forever unbreakable. But Juturna is whispering among the Rutulians that it is disgraceful, since they outnumber the Trojans, for them to let one man do their fighting for them. Even if he dies he will become famous, but they will be slaves.

At this critical moment a flock of wild swans is seen in the sky attacking an eagle which is trying to carry off one of them. The sheer weight of their numbers finally overpowers the bird of prey, and dropping the swan, he flies away into the clouds. Immediately this is interpreted as an omen that they should attack the Trojans.

One of the Rutilians casts a spear at the opposite side, and a wild free-for-all begins. The hail of javelins, spears and arrows is deadly. The solemn treaty, only minutes old, is worthless, and Latinus flees in despair. Some take up charred or burning sticks from the altar fire to hurl in the face of the nearest enemy. Others bash their opponents with battle-axes. In the center of the chaos stands Aeneas, bare-headed, shouting, in the vain attempt to get himself heard, that they must remember the treaty. His voice cannot possibly carry over the din, and his frantic gestures only serve to call attention to where he is. In a flash, an arrow from an unknown bow hits him in the knee. The hero becomes a martyr for the sake of law and order. He limps from the battle with blood streaming down his leg, while Turnus' spirits rise in a sudden surge of new confidence. He is more fierce than the very god of war himself as his horses trample the wounded under foot and the knife-blades on his chariot wheels cut men into ribbons. Completely forgetting the treaty, he creates havoc over the whole plain.

Meanwhile Aeneas' friends are franticly trying to stem the flow of blood from his knee, with virtually no success. Aeneas, paying no attention to the pain, works away at the barb of the arrow, but it has gone too deep and will not come out. Even the doctor, Iapyx, with all his knowledge of herbs, gets nowhere. So Venus must take matters in hand herself, and having cut a stalk of a plant which grew in Crete and was known for its healing power, she dips it into the water Iapyx is using to cleanse the wound. Immediately the flow is staunched, and the arrowhead comes out easily. The old doctor knows that a god has performed the miracle, but Aeneas hardly notices in his impatience to get back to the fighting. Filled with rage at the breach of the treaty, he drives over the battlefield like a mighty hurricane, sweeping everything before him. Tirelessly he seeks Turnus. But Juturna is guiding her brother's horses, and whenever it seems that he and Aeneas may meet, she drives them in the other direction. Hours after Aeneas searches for Turnus, killing only when he has to, and sparing those who flee for their lives. On his side, however, Turnus lusts for more and more blood as he stacks the heads of those he has killed, dripping with gore, on his chariot.

At last Aeneas gives up the chase temporarily and turns his energies to the walls and the high tower of Laurentum. Urging his soldiers on by the well-worn phrase that Jupiter is on their side, and determining to wait no longer for Turnus, he leads them with one accord in wedge formation up to the walls. Fires break out in a hundred different places at once. Scaling ladders are thrown up, the guards at the gates are cut down, clouds of smoke billow higher and higher. Poor queen Amata, thinking that the city is completely in the hands of her enemies and that Turnus is already dead, hangs herself in despair. The city resounds with the howling of women.

Comment

The various battle scenes in this book tumble one upon the other with such ever increasing speed that it is hard to find a pause. Of the two major actors, it is Turnus who commands our attention the most. His role is similar to Dido's in the fourth book, for both are controlled by passion. In this first portion of the last book death stalks in every line, but destiny is continually put off. Slowly, slowly, Turnus looses his confidence, which is first shaken by the tears of Lavinia and his mother. He goes forth to battle, not so much to win, as to fight and die nobly. Of his own free will he chooses glorious death if necessary, but the breach of the truce and the interference of his sister, Juturna, prevent it. Still, the atmosphere of tragic apprehension mounts as the Trojans attack the walls in disciplined formation, while within the city, all is panic.

NAMES AND PLACES

Agylla: small Etruscan town.

Dolon: Trojan spy, killed by Diomede. (*Iliad* X: 314 ff.)

Edoni: a people living in Thrace on the Strymon river.

Lynisus: a town in Asia Minor.

(LINES 614-952.)

Far in the distance, Turnus faintly hears the cries from the doomed city, and he begins to loose his zest for fighting. Filled with anxiety he determines to go back and to find out what has happened. Juturna, in her disguise as his charioteer, urges him to stay and fight where he is. The more Trojans he kills, the more famous he will be. But Turnus' eyes are opened and he recognizes his sister, in spite of her disguise. Full of reproaches he asks her what right she has to interfere. His luck has run out and the only hope left is that he may be spared any more humiliation, all because of meddling goddesses! 'At least let me win glory by dying nobly.'

At that moment a wounded Rutilian, Saces, gallops up shot through the face by an arrow, but valiantly determined to perform his duty. Though his face is contracted by pain his words confirm Turnus' horrible suspicions: the city is on the verge of collapse; the queen has committed suicide.

The words are a dagger in Turnus' heart. In anger he orders his sister to be gone. He will meet Aeneas now, and banish the shame that hangs over his name already. She may call it madness if she likes. His mind is made up. Like boulders broken loose from the top of a mountain leveling everything in their path, Turnus charges toward the city. Exultantly Aeneas sees him coming and thunders out to meet him. The din of swords clashing on shields is deafening. Turnus raises his sword high for the great blow, but it strikes the god-made shield of Aeneas... and snaps in two. Turnus leaps back in horror, looking at the broken weapon. Only then does he realize that the sword is not his own but his charioteer's which he snatched up by mistake. His own sword, made by Vulcan, would not have failed. Wildly he searches first for his own sword and then calls to his men for one of theirs, as Aeneas pursues him round the circle made by terrified Trojans and Rutilians.

Then Aeneas hurls his spear but it misses its mark and sticks fast in a clump of wild olive saplings. Turnus, catching his breath in this unlooked for delay, breathes a prayer to Faunus, the guardian spirit of the olive, to hold the spear fast so that Aenas may not be able to pull it out. And while Aeneas is tugging away with all his might, Juturna (still disguised as the charioteer) runs up to Turnus with his missing sword. Venus then gets angry that Juturna should have such power and comes down to free the spear for Aeneas. With the aid of the gods the odds are evened up again! Jupiter, too, ceases to be a spectator as he forbids Juno (for her power is behind Juturna's actions) to meddle any more: 'Is it not enough for her that she drove the Trojans over the sea, wrecked them on the shores of Carthage, and started this terrible war? What greater signs of power does she need, anyway? Juno must admit that he is right. And seeing that Turnus and his side are doomed she asks that the two sides become united under the Latin name and that the descendants be Romans, possessing the primitive strength of Italy. Let the name of Troy fall into oblivion. Jupiter promises that this wish shall be fulfilled. Juno is content, her wrath appeased at last. To remove Juturna from the scene the king of the gods sends one of the furies to drive her back to her fountain.

Now the end is near and both champions know it. They taunt each other with angry words, but Turnus says that it is not Aeneas who terrifies him, but the gods, for Jupiter is his enemy. The full realization of the truth of these words seems almost to paralyze him. He picks up a huge stone to heave at Aeneas but the throw is wild and comes nowhere near the hero. Loosing his senses he runs back and forth looking for a way to escape while Aeneas, choosing the right moment, hurls his spear like a shot from a catapult. Its head sinks deep into Turnus' thigh, and he falls to the ground.

A mighty groan up from the lips of the Rutilians, so loud that the whole hillside resounds with the echo. Not a sound comes from the Trojans. Turnus' last words are not a prayer for mercy, but rather an admission of his guilt: "I have deserved this. You have conquered; Lavinia is your wife." With these words he repeats the terms of the treaty. Half-heartedly he pleas for his life which Aeneas is ready to spare until he catches sight of the sword belt of Pallas which Turnus has worn ever since he killed the young man. Revenge and grief well up in his heart. Deep into the breast of his foe Aeneas plunges his sword and "with a groan, life fled to the underworld."

Comment

So the end comes to Turnus whose only crime was passion for honor. Yet he was guilty because it was this passion that caused him to start the war, and this passion that made him refuse to stop it. Almost to the last minute he is torn between the false hopes represented by Juno, Juturna, and Faunus, and his heart's desire, to save Italy for her native people, which he cannot abandon. But in the end he turns heroically to death to save his honor and performs a bitter penance by admitting his guilt to Aeneas. The book ends with Aeneas longing to spare Turnus, which is symbolic of Rome's great mission as expressed by Anchises in Book VI. But Turnus must die in order that peace, Rome's greatest gift to the world, may come.

NAMES AND PLACES

Cydonia: important city in Crete, rival of Knossos. Crete was famous for its archers.

SUMMARY

Book XII has three purposes: a.) to complete the picture of Turnus' character; b.) to give a final understanding of Aeneas; and c.) to emphasize the glory of Rome.

    a.   The reader is able to visualize Turnus because of the many similes.

        1. In the beginning he is compared to a lion slightly wounded, ready to attack the hunters. But he has lost some of the confidence which he possessed when we met him in Book IX.

        2. Then he is compared to a bellowing bull, charging a tree trunk. His efforts are futile because, though his nature is noble, his fighting passion has robbed him of sanity. This passion is symbolized by the appearance of the Fury at the beginning (Allecto, Book VII) and end (Megaera, Book XII) of his career.

        3. In the next **simile** he is not a beast, but Mars, the very god of war himself, driving his wild swift horses. Gradually, however, his strength decreases, **foreshadowing** the coming **catastrophe**. His words to Juturna indicate that he expects to die, but with honor. When he first comes on the scene in Book VII, he is sure of divine protection, for Juno is on his

side. In the end he says his destruction is due to the hatred of the gods.

4. Then he is compared to a plunging landslide, which hints at defeat.

5. In the final **simile**, he is a stag in terror of the hunting dogs and nets which are hemming him in. The important thing about his last words is not that he asks for his life, but that he admits his guilt. Virgil arouses the reader's compassion: as the fourth book ends with the tragedy of Dido, trapped by fatal passion and the interference of the gods (remember that Juno is the deity who represents passion throughout the *Aeneid*), so in the same way is Turnus trapped by his passion for honor and by the goddesses who prevent his achieving it; and his tragedy is nearly as great.

b. Aeneas in this book has become almost pure symbol, rather than a flesh and blood hero. Even in his similes, such as the one in which he is compared to a threatening storm, we do not see Aeneas the man so much as the psychological effects of his presence, and, above all, his personification of the Roman concepts of justice and order.

1. In his speech establishing the treaty he promises to "spare the conquered," but when the truce is broken, he must destroy his enemy to fulfill the mission of "crushing the proud."

2. For the sake of justice he is made a martyr, wounded by the unknown arrow, when he attempts to re-

establish law and order. It is in this instance that he represents the Roman ideal of waging war only in self-defense. He no longer glories in fighting. It has become a bitter necessity, forced upon him by his obligation to avenge Pallas, which is for Aeneas a duty.

3. He personifies order and civilization, too, when he and his disciplined troops attack Latinus' disorganized city.

4. At the end his tragic memory of Troy is gone forever. His personality has become so bound up with Rome's mission that he is the mythological symbol of her glory.

c. The triumph of Rome is seen in Aeneas defeating Turnus. For Aeneas represents the high ideal of Rome's laws and ethics, while Turnus stands for the natural strength of primitive Italy. The terms of the treaty with Latinus - that both nations would live together as equals - and the last wish of Juno - that the Roman race become powerful because of Italian virtue - symbolically express what Virgil believed: that the joining of these two forces, high ideals and primitive strength, in equal measure, is what produced the political and historical greatness of Rome.

CRITICISM

Critics have been discussing the *Aeneid* ever since the days of Virgil himself. It is impossible to include here everything that has been said. Perhaps of greater interest to the modern student is the change in understanding and appreciation of the poet's great work, the *Aeneid,* which has taken place in the nineteenth and twentieth centuries. In general it can be said that the nineteenth century approach (including the first twenty years or so of the twentieth century also) was one of either condemning Virgil for being inferior to Homer, or one of appreciating him in a sentimental or apologetic way. This criticism, in the words of Viktor Postil, the great modern German critic, was "blind to everything artistic", and "the sediment of a rationalism estranged from art and life." (page 5, the Art of Virgil; see list of works below.) On the other side, the modern critic realizes that art, and poetry is most certainly art, must be judged in relation to its own period in history, not in relation to the period in which the critic lives. A poet must be judged by how well he succeeds in the task he set himself, not in how well he succeeds in pleasing the reader. Scholars are now beginning to believe that Virgil must be understood, not so much as an imitator of Homer, but as a critic of Homer. They have given up the centuries old practice of trying to equate Homer and Virgil, or of putting them in the balance and finding one poet lacking.

Below is a list of some of the best known nineteenth and twentieth century scholars in the field, with their works, and their dates. The list includes one French name, Sainte-Beuve, and one German, Viktor Poschl. There are, of course, many more German scholars of the nineteenth century, but since their labors were mainly to condemn Virgil, they have not been included. Following the list of scholars are the various topics of criticism which most of the authors cover. The topics are illustrated by direct quotes from the works themselves in chronological order of when the books were written. Poschl's statements usually come last, for he typifies the modern approach. The reader should remember that all the statements represent the subjective appreciation of the various authors. Perhaps it would be a good idea to keep in mind the words of the famous British orator, Edmunde Burke, when he said in his Appeal from the New to the Old Whigs: "We ought not to follow our own fancies, but to study them (the great authors) until we know how and what to admire; and if we cannot arrive at this union of admiration with knowledge, rather to believe that we are dull than that the rest of the world has been imposed on."

CRITICS AND THEIR WORKS

Conington, John. *The Works of Virgil: vol. II*, George Bell & Sons, London, 1884. 1825-1869.

Duckworth, George Eckel. *Structural Patterns and Proportions in Virgil's Aeneid.* University of Michigan Press, Ann Arbor, 1962. (The quotes are taken from his article summarizing the book which appeared in *Transactions of the American Philological Association*, vol. 91, 1960, entitled "Mathematical Symmetry in the *Aeneid.*") 1903-.

Duff, John Wight. *A Literary History of Rome - the Golden Age.* Charles Scribner's Sons, New York, 1927. 1866-1944.

Glover, Terrot Reaveley. *Virgil*. Macmillan Co. New York, 1912. 1869-1943.

Knight, W. F. Jackson. *Roman Vergil*. Faber & Faber Ltd. London, 1944. 1895-.

Mackail, John William. *Virgil and His Meaning to the World of Today*. Marshall Jones & Co. London, 1922. 1859-1945.

Nettleship, Henry. *Suggestions Introductory to a Study of the Aeneid*. Clarendon Press, Oxford, 1875. Vergil. Appleton & Co. New York, 1880. 1839-1893.

Poschl, Viktor. (translated by Gerda Seligson) *The Art of Vergil*. University of Michigan Press, Ann Arbor, 1962. 1910-.

Sainte-Beuve, Charles Augustin. *Etude sur Virgile*. Paris, 1891. 1804-1869.

Sellar, William Young. *The Roman Poets of the Augustan Age-Virgil*. Clarendon Press, Oxford, 1908. 1825-1890.

RELATION TO HOMER

Sainte-Beuve: "The first book of the *Aeneid* is decked with Homer's most famous and conspicuous similes. Virgil displays and presents these at the beginning and in the most obvious places. Far from being embarrassed by this, he takes pride in it." (p. 107) "The immense moral force which emanates from so many of the tableaux of Homer appears more concentrated in Virgil, along with more reflection and in a mirror, so to speak, more clear cut and better defined." (p. 186) "The lesson of taste which one could obtain from it (the first book of the *Aeneid*) is not to admire Homer or Virgil less, but, as much as possible, to admire each in his own category and age of civilization." (p. 292)

Nettleship: "It can easily be imagined how often this devotion to the Greek **epic** has spoiled the freshness and spontaneousness of Vergil's writing. But in thus studying and using Homer as no Roman poet had studied and used him before, Vergil thought that he was doing no more than his duty to Latin literature (and he thought that) the never ceasing labor on the great master-piece of Greek literature to be the main condition of success in bringing Latin writing to perfection. --- Virgil's work has suffered by a too rigid adherence to the rules which he had laid down for himself." (Vergil: p. 68)

Sellar: "He can never again enter into rivalry with Homer as the inspired poet of heroic action." (p.78) "The interest which he imparts to his narrative is different from, and inferior to, that attaching to the original representation in the Homeric poems. --- Not only was Virgil's own genius much less creative than that of Homer, his materials possessed much less plasticity." (p. 394) "In employment of illustrative **imagery** Virgil is much more sparing than Homer." (p. 413) "Virgil's instrument fails, or at least is much inferior to Homer's in aptitude for natural dialogue or for bringing familiar things in the freshness of immediate impression before the imagination." (p. 419)

Glover: "Virgil has the poet's eye for human life, but he does not see it with Homer's freshness. It is partly because Homer has done or watched the things about which he writes, while Virgil has read about them in books and pictured them with the inner eye." (p. 48): "Virgil falls far short of Homer in expressing the stern joy that warriors feel." (p. 50).

Duff: "Some inapposite incidents and **similes** would not have been introduced but for the desire to emulate Homer." (p. 457) "To compensate for the absence of fire, he has exactitude of workmanship and equilibrium of style. --- "Virgil is more critical, urbane, emotional, than Homer." (p. 459) "With greater care for the proprieties there is less nature. Homer keeps the attention more closely, and is more fully believed. What reader can accept the legendary if it is artificially Romanized? --- He has not the imperturbable calm of Homer. --- Virgil is more humane; he is less simply human." (pp. 460-461)

Knight: uses the word "integrates" throughout his book to indicate the relationship of the two poets.

Poschl: "He added depth of feeling and symbolic significance to Homer's direct observations and literal meanings." (p. 3) "This is the central question for both aesthetic criticism and intellectual history, because when one compares Vergil with Homer, one compares --- two stages in the history of creative imagination." There is "a strange reenactment of Homer's poetry in the *Aeneid* and its preservation in the structure of a new work of art." (p. 7) "Vergil's attachment to Homer is akin to Roman reverence for the authority of traditional forms. --- According to the Roman point of view it is possible to create something perfect only by building on to something else which has itself grown slowly in the course of history. One must carry on and repeat past achievements in a new form. --- This exemplifies the peculiar Roman trait of not allowing something once found to be great and true to disappear, but to appeal to it again and again and thus to preserve it." (p. 8) "The crowning achievement of the Roman **epic** was made possible when for the first time Homer, the representative of Greek art and humanity, was absorbed by an equal. Vergil was Homer's peer in artistic greatness and emotional insight, discrimination, and passion." (p. 9) "The more openly he attests his dependence on Homer, the more ambitiously he strives to surpass him in the perfection of form and interpretation and connection of motifs." (p. 26) "Within the

Homeric shell lies the Virgilian kernel." (p. 28) "Loss of natural simplicity is the price paid for perfection of the classical form." (p. 36) Homer is "objective", and Vergil "subjective". (p. 40)

Duckworth: In the central part of the poem "long Homeric **episodes** (games, trip to underworld, catalogue, description of shield) are reworked for the glorification of Rome and its history, the portrayal of Ancient Italy, and the praise of Augustus and the new Golden Age." (p. 187)

POET OF WAR

Sellar: "In his scenes of battle Virgil is as inferior to Homer as he is in portraying sea adventure. (p. 388)

Duff: "Virgil does not enjoy the slayings any more than his reader; he is merely overborne by convention." (p. 458)

Poschl: "Rather than banishing Homer's **realism** from his work, Vergil has toned it down and transfigured it through his art. --- The horrors of war had to be shown - that the strength and glory of Rome might shine all the more." (p. 100) "On the other hand Vergil's scenes (of war) lack the powerful vitality and primitive strength of the Greek epic." (p. 101)

CHARACTER OF AENEAS

Sellar: " --- Aeneas is altogether wanting in energy, spontaneity, intellectual resource, and insight." (p. 397) "He undergoes no passionate struggle in resigning Dido." (p. 398) "He is the passive receptacle of Divine guidance." (p. 399)

Duff: "Dutiful to his old father and to the gods, --- his desertion of Dido---leaves Aeneas either more or less than human, --- either demigod, or brute. (p. 463) "Aeneas is too often a puppet." (p. 464)

Poschl: Aeneas is the "personification of things Roman" (p. 16); "he realizes the connection of mortal life with world order and that of his own destiny with the history of Rome." (p. 27) "a man of memory and inner vision" (p. 35); he has "compassion for Dido's grief." (p. 44) "He suffers more for the sorrows of others than because of his own misfortune." (p. 44) He is "compassionate." (p. 51) He "prefigures the Christian hero whose heart remains gentle through struggle and sorrow and beats in secret sympathy with all suffering creatures." (p. 53) He "experiences spiritual sorrow to the utmost." (p. 54) He is a man of tragedy because of the "conflict of heroic fulfillment of duty with human sensitivity." (p. 58) He "potentiality for experiencing sorrow grows with the realization of the greatness of his task." (p. 59)

SPIRITUAL ELEMENT

Sainte-Beuve: "He makes us believe, by the serious sweetness of his words, by the pure light which emanates from his work and his genius, in something polished, brilliant, generally enlightening, in something humane and almost holy." (p. 68) "Virgil, like his hero, has both a quality of piety and pity, occasionally, a touch of sadness, of almost melancholy." (p. 100)

Sellar: "And though the representation of the outward world in Virgil is, in its serene beauty, suggestive of a secret unceasing life which appeals to the human spirit in its more tranquil moods, yet it does not move the mind to that profounder sense of an affinity between the soul of man and the soul of Nature which the great modern poets awaken." (p. 88) "Virgil produces the most powerful effect by the use of simplest words in their simplest application. They affect the mind with a strange potency, of which perhaps no account can be given except that they make us feel - the burden of the mystery of life, and by their marvelous beauty, the reflection, it may be, from some light dimly discerned or imagined beyond the gloom, they make it seem more easy to be borne." (p. 423)

Mackail: "In none is there so deep a sense of the beauty and sorrow of life, of keen remembrances and shadowy hope, and enfolding all, of infinite pity." (p. 110)

Duff: "Virgil is spiritual, touched with doctrine, reverie, regrets, misgivings, consecration --. His brooding melancholy he wedded mystically to this strong confidence in the service which his country must render to the world. --- His regard for things of the spirit struck harmonious chords in early Christian hearts --." (p. 462) "Virgil's tender melancholy is merged in his profound reflections. He both thought and felt deeply on life." (p. 469)

Poschl: "Aeneas suffers for the sake of others. A new humanity announcing the Christian philosophy burst forth from him" (p. 53) "Virgil infused the Roman idea of duty with deep humanity, (bringing) it closer to the Christian idea of charity and solidarity." (p. 54) He has a "reverence for the mystery of fate." (p. 73) He believed in "a divine plan controlling and directing universal events." (p. 73) "He emphasizes pain through a reference to joy, darkness through light, and failure through a final triumph." (p. 172) "Vergil expresses a religious feeling which precludes the isolation of any one part of life. --- Every single thing has a place in a divine world where glory and gloom, reason and emotion, demonic and divine, are restricted and reinforced through their opposites." (p. 173)

HANDLING OF SIMILES

Sellar: "Another class of **similes** --- merely give a realistic outward symbol of some movement of the mind or passions without any imaginative enhancement of the situation." (p. 414)

Poschl: Homer "aims at illumination of visible relations while Vergil aims to establish moods, interpret states of mind, and to intimate impending fate. --- sergilian **similes** are --- more felt than observed." (p. 81) He connected his **similes** "most intimately with the interior action which accompanies the exterior events." (p. 65) "Their function is to give the poem depth ---." (p. 66) "In Vergil's hands the **simile** is a deeply integrated whole, highlight and focal point for unfolding events. It is a bold and beautiful picture of the idea and destiny of **epic** heroes." (p. 99) "Homer usually concludes his **similes** with a concrete detail which adds nothing material to what precedes it. Vergil concludes his **similes** with an image that satisfies the musical requirement for a beautiful chord." (p. 161)

CENTRAL IDEA OF POEM

Sainte-Beuve: In the *Aeneid* we see that "triumph is always incomplete, unachieved, and mixed with shadow; these are the miseries of even victory, the sad resemblance and almost equality of the conquerors and the conquered ---." (p. 186)

Nettleship: "The primary purpose of the *Aeneid* --- is --- not so much to delineate 'character' as to exhibit the conflict of forces." (Suggestions: p. 36) "The *Aeneid* is therefore a poem of which the main idea is Roman, the mythology a bastard mixture of Greek and Italian, and the arrangement and handling wholly Greek." (Vergil: p. 61)

Duff: "His central idea is to uphold the new monarchy as one foreshadowed in the fatherly leadership of Aeneas, and predestined to follow the long and glorious evolution of the republic. It is a historic idea majestic in its historic associations. It flattered the national pride, but it did not stir the heart." (p. 465)

Poschl: The basic **theme** of the poem is "the struggle and final victory of order. --- The demonic appears in history as civil or foreign war, in the soul as passion, and in nature as death and destruction. Jupiter, Aeneas, and Augustus are its conquerors, while Juno, Dido, Turnus, and Antony are its conquered representatives." (p. 18) "The *Aeneid* is a poem of humanity, not a political manifesto. In it, myth and history acquire meaning and grandeur as expression of a higher level, the realization of a divine order, the symbol of the cosmic law of destiny revealed in the existence of the world of man." (p. 23)

Duckworth: "The **epic** rises far above the patriotic and historical level in the poet's dramatic treatment of character and event, and in his introduction of loftier **themes** of philosophy and religion; it is an **epic** not only of Rome but of human life as well." (p. 185) "The *Aeneid* is the story of Aeneas but it is also the story of the destiny of Rome under Augustus. This latter provides much of the central core of the poem (V-VIII) and concludes with the victories and triumphs of Augustus as described on the shield at the end of VIII." (p. 186)

ART AND STYLE

Sainte-Beuve: "Virgil, from the hour when he appeared has been the poet of Latinity in its entirety. He gave a new form to taste, to passion, and to sensitivity." (p. 1) "When a poet has the talent and the artistic skill to express thus the present and actual feelings of his nation, to exalt the feeling of its dominion and its triumph, and also to reflect and paint distant horizons and incredibilities of remotest times, and unites all these, he does not fail to delight, and to elevate his century for posterity." (p. 79)

Conington: "In undertaking the *Aeneid* at the command of a superior, Virgil was venturing beyond the province of his genius." (Introduction to vol. II. page xix.)

Nettleship: " --- Virgil was able by his wonderful power of style to produce work which marks the **climax** of a particular kind of poetry, which completes and embodies in itself much that preceding poets had been striving after, and which gave the law to succeeding generations of writers." (Vergil: p. 1) "His genius was fitted more for the elaboration of detail than for the clear grasping of general conceptions." (Vergil: p. 98)

Sellar: "The *Aeneid* as an **epic** poem representative of the Roman Empire -- does not touch the heart or enlighten the conscience: and this is an important drawback to the claim which the *Aeneid* may have to the highest rank as a work of art." (p. 354) "In the *Aeneid* Virgil's style appears as great in its power of reaching the secrets of the human spirit as in the *Georgics* it proved itself to be in eliciting the deeper meaning of Nature." (p. 421)

Duff: "To compensate for the absence of fire he has exactituted of workmanship and equilibrium of style." (p. 459) "Words are combined with theme so that the Virgilian musings, descriptions, speeches, rich in a compassionate tenderness, attain the finished beauty of a solemn music." (p. 470) "The beauty of Virgil's style was produced by a minute and sedulous shaping of words in the endeavor to satisfy the imperious demands of a refined self-criticism and an ear divinely attuned --- Virgil's ideal was the choice of words which in themselves and in association are winsome, impressive, and worthy of a noble theme." (p. 477) "Under Virgil's verbal sorcery, Latin becomes a golden language of exquisite richness, veined with a delicate melancholy, and wistful reverie upon the abundant travail of life." (p. 478)

Knight: "There is layer on layer of thought and emotion, coinciding marvelously in the end. The chief layers are the forms and contents of Greek poems - current thought and feeling and symbolism of Vergil's own time - the Roman tradition of history guided by destiny, and the historical or legendary conditions and events of the Mediterranean world at the end of the age of bronze, and of Italy in the earlier centuries of Rome." (p. 100)

Poschl: "One of the most important principles of Vergil's art (is) the striving for unity." (p. 31) The "preference for 'grandeur,' 'pathos,' and the 'sublime' is a marked characteristic of Vergil's style." (p. 142) "With consummate artistry, Vergil has made --- landscape fit the mood and character of --- action." (p. 142) "Since Vergil, 'mood' has become to poetry what 'light' is to painting --- Vergil's poem is a stream of moods and feelings blended delicately together and which move the heart with melody and lead from one emotional quality to another." (p.

156) " --- sequence of mood --- is the core of the narrative. Viewed as a whole, it proceeds in a swelling and ebbing motion or in recurring waves." (p. 157) "Throughout the poem there is a rhythmic pattern of light and shadow." (p. 165) "Vergil's aesthetic concept, like all Classical concepts, postulates the harmonious balance of opposites." (p. 173)

Duckworth: There are three structural patterns: "1) the alternation of the books, those with even numbers being of a more serious and tragic nature than those with odd numbers which are lighter and serve to relieve the tension; 2) parallelism by similarity and contrast between books in each half, I and VII, II and VIII etc.; 3) a tripartite division of the **epic** into three groups of four books each --- It is thus a trilogy with the first four books the tragedy of Dido, and the last four books and tragedy of Turnus, enclosing in a framework pattern the central portion, where long Homeric **episodes** --- are reworked --- for the glorification of Rome --- and the praise of Augustus and the new Golden Age." (pp. 186 ff.) He goes on to say that the individual books within the poem are based on tripartite divisions of major and minor episodes. The number of lines in the major and minor passages can be shown to have a mathematical ratio of approximately .618. This was the number known to the ancients as the Golden Section, or the Golden Mean. If we let m equal the number of lines in the minor **episode**, and M equal the number of lines in the Major **episode**, we would have the following statement:

m / M as M / (m + M)

An example would be a group of lines in Book III. The shorter passage is from line 1 - 191 (m = 191); the longer is 192 - 505 (M = 310.8 because there are some incomplete lines and he rounds these to a per cent = 310.8 / 501.8 = .6185. (pp. 192 - 198; he goes into considerably more detail than this.) This suggests that Vergil wishes the listener to be conscious of the mathematical symmetry of the poem or to derive a subconscious pleasure from the harmony of the proportions." (p. 201)

ORIGINALITY

Nettleship: "His imitations seem crude, obvious, often inappropriate." Suggestions: p. 27) "The Roman poets were still simple enough to think that open imitation was rather a grace than a defect." (Suggestions: p. 29)

Sellar: "Virgil's power as an **epic** poet does not consist in original invention of incident or action, but in combining diverse elements into a homogeneous whole, and imparting poetic life to old materials, many of them not originally conceived in a poetic spirit." (p. 394)

Duff: "The originality of Virgil is most manifest where he is most natural." (p. 461) "To minimize his creative gifts - either on the ground of his borrowing of conventions, as if he were a second-hand plagiarist, or on the ground of his conscious aim, as if he overdid the **didactic** - is to miss the significance of Virgil's relation to his age." (p. 482)

Knight: "The success of Vergil is partly due to his willed or spontaneous, perhaps unconscious patience - in waiting till the wealth of his thought and feeling and observation, much of it directly taken from the contemporary world, gathered sufficient literary and traditional material to frame or mold or constrain, and so make artistic and universal, all that his keen artistic and practical vigilance had acquired." (p. 145)

Poschl: "In Vergil's poetry everything participates in the inner drama and reflects the poet's awareness of the stirrings within the souls of his characters and of the destiny inherent in the events. Everything-landscape, morning, evening-movement and image becomes a symbol of the soul. The cadence of each line radiates an inner light and shimmers with nuances of feeling --- It is easily seen how much of what was inexpressible before is now within the range of expression and how great a debt later poets owe Vergil. In this light it seems more than foolish to doubt Vergil's ' originality.' Such doubt arises from a profound misunderstanding of Vergil's poetry and of artistic creativity in general." (p. 3) "His critics and his apologists, influenced by the obvious borrowings, overlooked the decisive changes beneath the surface. This may serve as a warning against the type of interpretation which almost always tacitly assumes that Vergil simply appropriated the content of older works along with the motifs, be it in relation to Homer-or Naevius and Ennius. He did not do that! The secret of his originality is hidden in the transformation, connection, and deepening of the motifs to which he gave another meaning and a new beauty. He did this through sensitive changes, through a web of mysterious references, through novel light and sound effects. Such artistry with line and color, composition and combination, is the very nature of his poetry. In a word, it is the form through which a new soul emerges as if by magic from the borrowed material. An inner readiness, a loving, if critical contemplation, is needed to recognize it." (p. 68)

. . . .

Question: Why read Virgil?

Answer: There are many answers to this question, but one of the most important is that he, more than any other poet, established the ascendency of Roman culture (and thus Greek culture because the Roman incorporated the Greek) and ideas in the history of Western thought. The *Aeneid* was a "classic" as soon as it was published, and Virgil's influence grew greater rather than diminished in succeeding generations. He was one of the few classic authors well known throughout the period of the "Dark" and "Middle" ages. This was due primarily to the tremendous spiritual side of his poetry and the sonorous music of the lines. A knowledge of Virgil's poetry deepens immeasurably our ability to appreciate the great poets of the Renaissance, such as Dante, Dryden, Milton, or Shakespeare. His work can truly be considered, in Poschl's words: "one of the bibles of the Western world." (*The Art of Virgil*: p. 12).

Question: What do Virgil's works reveal about his philosophy?

Answer: Virgil was a deep thinker. Even his earliest works show this. But his ideas changed somewhat as he grew older. In his youth he was more of an idealist. To a certain degree, he really believed in the possibility of a Golden Age as the exalted tones of the fourth Eclogue show. He was influenced by the Epicurean idea of science as the explanation for the universe, of tranquility through knowledge, and of the steady progress of mankind. These ideas appear most strongly in the *Georgics.* At the same time the *Georgics* have a certain Stoic element as well as Epicurean, with their emphasis on duty and hard work, and a suggestion of a divine spirit permeating the universe. The *Georgics* also contain many traces of Virgil's more youthful belief in and longing for the Golden Age. But in this later work he is much less certain that it will come. The Golden Age is an ideal in the *Georgics.* In the *Eclogues* it is a possible reality.

The *Aeneid* is the great proponent of Stoic doctrine. It stresses respect for character, belief in divine ordering of the world, a sense of duty, and inner strength which gives control over fortune. It also emphasizes the concept of a unity of the cosmos and the state. But Virgil was more than an adherent to a particular brand of philosophy. Like any man searching for spiritual truths, he held to some concepts and rejected others. The Epicurean explanation of atoms and void combining to create everything in the universe did not satisfy answers to questions about love, endurance, or that greatest of all Roman virtues, pietas (loving and willing performance of one's duty to ancestors, parents, the gods and the state). Virgil believed in a universe divinely created and controlled according to laws, both physical and moral. But he did not define the degree to which free will and divine guidance can exist side by side. A spiritual element exists in all of Virgil's works, and ultimately every person who reads with a searching mind will find something relevant to his own outlook on life.

Question: What are the major **themes** of the *Aeneid?*

Answer: First and foremost, the *Aeneid* is a poem symbolizing Rome's destiny. Virgil had a passionate conviction in the greatness of Rome. The belief was not implanted in him by order from Augustus. It came from within his own soul. This greatness, which Virgil believed came to pass because of the joining of high ideals with primitive strength, was manifest in the past in the struggle with the Italian tribes (which covered many generations of Roman history) and later with Carthage. The struggle with Carthage is symbolized in Book IV where Aeneas is finally victorious over his feelings for Dido. The struggle with the Italian tribes is symbolized in the hero's final conquering of Turnus. These are examples of the great **theme** : the struggle and final victory of order. There is also the **theme** of the symbolic relationship between nature and politics, myth and history. This included the concept that Roman order was founded in the divine whole; pietas was its greatest virtue. A third **theme** is the idea of tragedy - the tragedy of human life and Roman history because of the conflict between duty and desire. Yet in spite of the awareness of tragedy, the *Aeneid* is a poem of hope, hope that order will conquer chaos, and that out of suffering will come peace and joy.

Question: What is the purpose of Virgil's similes?

Answer: The main purpose of Virgil's **similes** is to create mood and atmosphere, and show how the characters feel. They establish not so much a visual picture as a mental image of a person's state of mind. They also serve to suggest impending fate. For these reasons they add not just a pictorial quality but a spiritual depth to the poem.

Question: What is the role of the gods in the *Aeneid?*

Answer: The gods play a double role. They are connected directly with the action in the plot, partly from the **epic convention** of having the gods take part in the story, but more important, as illustrating the idea that there is a divine plan controlling history. Every historical event has two levels: one is the human level with its desires and intentions; the other is the divine, which manipulates these events. The second role of the gods is to symbolize the various aspects of human character. Jupiter, the king of the gods, is a symbol of man's ability to organize and control himself both mentally and physically. Juno, the queen of the gods, is a symbol of the opposite elements, such as anger, which causes a person to lose control of himself and the situation. Jupiter has power (potestas) because he has control. The role of Venus, the goddess of love, is one of a protectress and a calm, reassuring influence; not of exciting to passion, strange as this may seem. This is basically because she is the mother of Aeneas. Her importance in the story is due to her motherhood, not her divinity. Thus the divine and human are interwoven throughout the poem, with Jupiter as the ruler of both.

Question: Why are there two ways of spelling Virgil's name?

Answer: The poet's name is spelt with an e in all the early imperial inscriptions and in the earliest and best manuscripts of his works. There is evidence that there was a certain amount of fluctuation in spelling during the last century of the Republic, but the poet refers to himself as Vergilius. Possibly due to the change in pronunciation, his name came to be commonly spelt with an i by the fifth century A.D. This spelling continued during the Middle Ages and the Renaissance. It was also the general spelling in the nineteenth century. Recently, however, scholars are trying to go back to the Ver spelling since it is recognized as the correct one from the manuscripts.

BIBLIOGRAPHY AND GUIDE TO FURTHER RESEARCH

Bailey, Cyril. *Religion in Virgil,* Clarendon Press, Oxford, 1935.

Comparetti, Domenico (trans. by E.F.M. Benecke). *Virgil in the Middle Ages,* the Macmillan Co., New York, 1908.

Connington, John and Nettleship, Henry. *The Works of Virgil* (2 vols.) George Bell and Sons, London; 1858. 1884.

Duckworth, George Eckel. *Structural Patterns and Proportions in Vergil's Aeneid.* University of Michigan Press, Ann Arbor, 1962.

Frank, Tenney. *Vergil, a Biography.* Clarendon Press, Oxford, 1922.

Glover, T. R. *Virgil,* the Macmillan Co., New York, 1912.

Highet, Gilbert. *Poets in a Landscape,* Alfred A. Knopf, New York, 1957.

Knight, W. F. Jackson. *Roman Virgil,* Faber & Faber, Ltd., London, 1953.

Letters, F. J. H. *Virgil,* Sheed & Ward, New York, 1946.

Mackail, J. W. *Virgil and his Meaning to the World of Today,* Marshall Jones Co., Boston, 1922.

Nettleship, Henry. *Suggestions Introductory to a Study of the Aeneid,* Clarendon Press, Oxford, 1875. Vergil. Appleton & Co., New York, 1880.

Nitchie, Elizabeth. *Vergil and the English Poets.* Columbia University Press, New York City, 1919.

Oxford Classical Dictionary, Clarendon Press, Oxford; 1957.

Poschl, Victor (trans. by Gerta Seligson). *The Art of Vergil.* University of Michigan Press, Ann Arbor, 1962.

Prescott, Henry W. *The Development of Virgil's Art,* University of Chicago Press, Chicago, 1927.

Rand, Edward Kennard. *The Magical Art of Virgil.* Harvard University Press, Cambridge, 1931.

Sellar, William Young. *The Roman Poets of the Augustan Age - Virgil.* Clarendon Press, Oxford, 1908.

Smith, William and Anthon, Charles. *A New Classical Dictionary.* Harper Bros., New York, 1851.

Syme, Ronald. *The Roman Revolution.* Clarendon Press, Oxford, 1939.